Wild Nights.

Wild Nights

How to Ace the High School and College Essay

Wild nights – Wild nights!
Were I with thee
Wild nights should be
Our luxury!

- Emily Dickinson

About the Author: Chip Lee has taught college and high school English in California and Colorado since 1986. He has presented his writing approach at many English and Language Arts conferences, and is the author of a biography entitled *On Edge: The Life and Climbs of Henry Barber*, as well as having published verse in several journals. This is the third edition of *Wild Nights*. Chip has also been a charter pilot, flight instructor, ski instructor, mountain guide, squash pro, fitness club manager, and chimney sweep. He received a B.A. from Hampshire College and an M.A. in English literature from the University of Colorado. He lives in Boulder with his wife Cathy, has two grown kids, and spends his time climbing as much as possible.

Cover Image: Istock.com, 2016
Cover Design and Layout: Anne-Claire Siegert and Renee Rockford

ISBN-13: 978-1532821721
ISBN-10: 1532821727

Acknowledgements:

Thanks to my wife, Cathy, for supporting over ten years of work on this third edition of *Wild Nights*—the ups and the downs, and the constant belief and encouragement. Thanks to the ten student writers who appear in this book—the endless drafting they did—usually well upwards of a half-dozen rewrites. Also thanks to the students who wrote essays that appeared in or were considered for the book's earlier two renditions. Thanks, in general, to all the motivated students—those who really care—with whom I've worked. I am indebted to the people who took time to read and help with formatting the manuscript: Renee Rockford for invaluable finishing and design work, Anne-Claire Siegert for In-Design work; Jan Beattie and Emily Perez for serious formatting help; Luis Terrazas, Stuart Mills, Brett James, Juliana Rodriguez, and Bill Briggs for reading and commenting; and especially Anne Strobridge, who put in insane amounts of time over these many years to edit, road-test, and encourage the idea. Thanks to all of the smaller helps, mostly from colleagues at school, especially the tech department; the list of all the smaller helps could go on for many pages. Lastly, I think about central people who made me want to write and teach: Marty Bickman, Ed Nolan, Robert Meredith, David Smith, Jeff Long, John Krakauer, and especially Bruce Boston of San Diego who still teaches me today—"Vivas!"

TABLE of CONTENTS

Student Introduction

Short, concise, and easy to read: that's the principle of this book.

Written for you, the student, this guide recognizes your harried life. You don't have a lot of time to read even more than you already do in class. You need it short and direct; you need it easy to read; you need it to deliver the information without a lot of extra detail or teacher-speak. You need, finally, a simplification of a process that often seems mysterious and abstract, with different instructors giving you different rules.

Most of all, you probably just need a method that will work in all of your classes across the board. Well, here you go.

A teacher or a class is not required to make sense of these eight easy-to-follow steps, and you'll see the results by the time you turn in your first paper. Just follow the steps, don't skip any, and then look up what you don't understand or ask an expert. Again, the principle here is ease and brevity—something you'll actually read—so there are parts that you might want to fill in with some further research.

You're probably starting this book mid-way through an academic writing career in which you've been taught various ways of completing an essay. However, these many instructors have one outcome in mind: a clear, concise, and analytical paper. You'll see here many of the elements of what you've been taught, but everything you really need to know about writing, no matter what the course, appears here in its most stripped-down form. A little tweak here and there in the method and you'll satisfy any of the requirements of any class.

Most of my work as a teacher who's graded papers for thirty years, both high school and university, is in de-mystifying the writing process. It's not rocket science—just basic principles of communication that you use every day, in and out of class. So toss your writing preconceptions, and, with an open mind, begin practicing these techniques that will see you from high school papers all the way to journalism, business, and even love letters, should they be written any more.

Teacher Introduction

"JUST TELL ME HOW TO DO IT"

I can't tell you how many times I've heard that request in my thirty years of teaching. When it comes to writing papers, most students crave a formula, a recipe for writing success. They want to be told, "Just follow these steps and you'll ace that paper."

There are many amazing writing handbooks out there that teach students to think of themselves as writers—that break down writing into its most finite parts. This is not one of those books, *nor* is this intended to replace those books. I have always, and will continue to insist that all of my students purchase certain writing handbooks that you'll find in the bibliography at the end of this book.

The approach here, different from any other how-to guide, is designed to give students a process. Start here. Then do this. And now this. That is what my students are constantly looking for—a formula, a method, a progression. So I developed this eight-step approach.

This book is the absolute minimum—something utterly stripped-down and simple. I've kept as much theory out of the book as possible. Some of it creeps in, but generally only so students can follow the method.

A Few Notes Worth Mentioning:

The essays in this book are written about books and poems that are widely anthologized and assigned in both high school and undergraduate English/Language Arts courses. This handbook is for both high school and college level writers.

An efficient way to use this book in class is by having students read one of the eight initial sections in Part One per day. Students can be walked through the models in Part Two to see examples of each of the eight steps.

The editing checklists at the end of Part One are instantly applicable to any essay for any class. The checklists work especially well in group settings.

The models in Part Two are arranged by category. Some are written on themes, or subjects, while others are based on close reading or secondary sources. See the Introduction for Part Two to determine category.

A useful assignment is to have students write an essay following exactly the form of one of the models: the same paragraph structures, the same length, the same approach to the conclusion, the same attention to specific portions of text. Some teachers have assigned essays that ask students to borrow words, transitions, topic sentences, and last lines from the essays (with the appropriate citations). The aim in such writing is to have students learn how these structures were accomplished in the essays, and why.

Mostly, the essays will allow a teacher to show students how to handle, say, "theme," or "tone," or "close reading." These are essays to which a teacher can point when rehearsing an upcoming essay. Now you can say, "Hey, I want it like this."

The Eight Basic Steps –
An Overview of Strong Writing

Step 1: CHOOSE YOUR VOICE

Decide whether you should use your own plain one or the technical jargon of that academic field. Your instructor will make it clear as to which one.

Step 2: SHOW THAT YOU HAVE READ

The key word here is *evidence*: the facts. Either you have the facts or you don't. Evidence = facts = text = your command over the class material.

Step 3: FIGURE OUT YOUR TOPIC

Coming up with your argument —your thesis—is about looking at a specific piece of text. Examine the facts and choose that specific piece of text that will become the topic of your essay.

Step 4: FIND YOUR ARGUMENT – THE POINT YOU'LL MAKE

The format of your essay is based optimally on *one argument*—a point you want to make. Essay structure—its sequence—proceeds from the argument you want to make—your interpretation of the facts.

Step 5: WRITE THE FIRST DRAFT

This first writing is where you just hammer it out, as fast as you can, without editing, without thinking, and without outlining. This is where you find out and then watch yourself come to ideas.

Step 6: SORT IT OUT

After you've gotten the lump-sum of your thinking down on paper, probably totally disorganized, you'll go back through and a) locate the point you appear to be after, and b) figure out a form and a structure for the essay.

Step 7: REWRITE THE DRAFT

Now you know the definitive argument/point that you want to make and you have a sorted-out draft. It's time to begin the final copy—a new document in itself.

Step 8: CHECK IT OVER

Lastly, it's imperative that you spend the extra go-through time, checking a) style, b) grammar, and c) mechanics.

A Word About PLAGIARISM

An instructor reading a plagiarized paper requires about ten milliseconds to pick up on the imported, not-you words, phrases, and concepts. We who have read 10,000+ papers can read a plagiarized paper "written" by someone we've never even met and we can pick up the discrepancies; it usually takes about five sentences to condemn the "writer" to the lowest circle of Dante's hell.

1.   The chances of being caught are much higher than most students think.

2.   When you plagiarize, you divorce yourself from the good will that is the honest dialogue happening in that particular classroom—a destructive process all around.

3.   Your transcript and your prospects may well tank.

4.   Most every institution now uses a plagiarism filter, so your chances of being picked up are extremely great. This book, for example, is already in every database that detects plagiarism, so it would be unwise to copy an essay out of the Models section in Part Two. Your instructor, too, has a plagiarism filter in her head, so consider the problem of raising that person's suspicions. Most people, once they think they've heard a lie, usually can't get it out of their heads.

5.   And if those don't do it, remember that you will wake up every day for the rest of your life with that perhaps-miniscule-speck of doubt about what and who you are. Plagiarizing in most cases is a choice, and while we might remember most of our good decisions, we always, always, always remember what we regret. T.S. Eliot, the great poet,

said in various ways that regret is, flat out, the dominant human emotion: "Time is no healer," he said so rightly. Ok, maybe that's pessimistic, but if you think about your past, you'll probably agree with him. So don't complicate your future.

6.   To make sure that you don't inadvertently plagiarize or mis-cite, ask, ask, ask if you have the slightest doubt. No instructor alive will fault you for coming in and asking. So many students get tagged because they thought they were paraphrasing, but here's a rule:

6a.   There's no such thing as paraphrasing; you're either citing sources or not, period.

7.   It's really the state of your soul that's at stake here.

Go ask your professor about where you are on that fine line when you "import text" or get a friend's help. There's no penalty—ever—for asking. Rather, your professor will applaud and help you. Your good curiosity, forthrightness, and effort are what your teachers are really after and what could mean the benefit of the doubt when it comes to your grade.

Step 1:
Choose Your Voice

Before you can even get to the paper, you have to identify the voice that your professor wants to see in your writing. There are only two options here: your actual, speaking voice, or the jargon of that field you're studying. Better than 50% of your classes are going to require you to write in a technical "institutional" language.

Here is an example of jargon from some literary theory:

"The ideological critique does not depend on some dogmatic or 'positive' conception of Marxism as a system. Rather, it is simply the place of an imperative to totalize, and the various historical forms of Marxism can themselves equally effectively be submitted to just such a critique of their own local ideological limits or strategies of containment." (Frederic Jameson, quoted from *Modern/Postmodern*, by Silvio Gaggi, 1989; p. 181)

Let's translate the above into plain voice:

"Whenever a reader uses a particular system of thought—for example, Marxism—to make sense of a text, that reader risks seeing things in a limited way—as just black or white, this or that."

Before the first class of the term has concluded, you'll know if this instructor wants jargon or your voice.

You use your spoken voice to make a convincing and forceful point, as when you talk to people, telling them stories or voicing your opinions. Look at magazine articles or blogs: you'll hear the spoken voice, not jargon. Read, read, read; then model your own voice after your favorite writers.

Your persuasive voice is based on one principle: BE HONEST. That means, you absolutely must have a connection to what you write; you have to want to write it. It's what you need to write. You have to care. This has to be something that you want to say, not just an assignment that you slog through. Slogging produces a monotonic, false voice, one that says to the grader that you're just trying to get it in and get that grade. Real writers care about what they write.

Finding Your Natural Voice

Here's how to achieve your own, unique voice: WRITE OUT LOUD. Speak your writing. Your hand should just be copying down what you're saying. In conversations with friends, you don't speak in jargon; you speak as *you*. For great writing, just listen to your own words. There should never be silence in your head—rather, the sound of you talking to your computer.

Never write silently.

Step 2:
Show That You've Read

Use of evidence is the main thing we look for when we grade anything you've written. Teachers want, bottom line, to know that you have actually read the whole book, listened to the lectures, and participated in the recitation groups. It's pretty clear—instantly—when someone has just skimmed or read the online notes.

Evidence IS...
Actual words that appear in the book
Actual events and actions that occur in the book
Actual people doing things in the book

Evidence is NOT...
Commonplace ideas like "freedom" or "moral" or "truth." A commonplace in writing—a broad concept, often used in politics, not even close to defined—indicates that the writer is either clueless or evasive. Beware.

Is some evidence better than others? How do you choose it? Easy—you have one of two kinds of professors: the kind that wants you to give back certain information and concepts, or the one who wants you to push both creativity and originality. The former makes sense in med school, and the latter makes sense in English lit. However, be aware that many humanities teachers will require you to give back exactly what they have told you.

If it's the sort of teacher who requires specific information/concepts in a statistics, communications, or maybe a history course, then problem solved. Begin and stick with the evidence you have from your lecture notes or the class website.

If it's the other sort of teacher, the one who wants you to push your own thinking some more, in an English, philosophy, or maybe again a history course, then you select your evidence by how well you feel you can explain it. You get some parts and don't get others. If you write about what you don't know, you're heading for problems. **Go with your strengths.**

Step 3:
Figure Out Your Topic

There are two ways in which every instructor assigns an essay:

Open-Topic Paper: Here, you choose the topic and create the thesis (or argument that you'll make) and interpretation.

Essay Prompt: In this form, you are given a question or a statement to which you reply.

Open-Topic Paper

Open papers present you with the seemingly insoluble problem of, "What the heck am I going to write about?" The one thing you need to know right now is that writing about the entire book, the entire article, the entire compendium of events, is automatic failure. We only understand the whole thing by looking at a part of it—just one thing at a time, not all of it. So, what do you write about? The answer is always the same: a very specific piece of text—a line, a moment, an action.

The easiest way to find that *right* argument in the text is to go ahead and—*quickly*, before you can doubt yourself—write down a list of scenes or moments that best explain what this book is all about. Fast, from your gut, and don't be thinking about whether they are "bad" or "good."

Essay Prompt

In a prompt, you're given a direction in which to head, but your job is the same as with an open paper: you have to be writing on a specific piece of text—a subject, an event, an action, a line. Prompts are just a little easier because of the nudge they give you into a particular area of discussion. However, most prompts can lead you to generalizing about huge concepts across the entirety of the work. Don't get sucked in; stay tightly focused on one specific piece of text.

Tips for Essay / Test Prompts

If you have been given a prompt on which to write, here is the approach:

1.   **Answer the question and only the question.** You are not given license to depart from the question.
2.   **Answer the question but do not repeat the question.** It's an adage used in all grading. In other words, no parroting back what we have all just read; cut right to your argument *in the text*.
3.   **Choose a "thing."** Write on scratch paper the one moment (or event or phrase) from the text—or a short list of them—that most relates to the question itself.
4.   **Address all parts.** As there are usually multiple subordinate parts of the prompt, make sure to come up with a scene, moment, or event that is coupled with each question-part. There are usually two or three "sub-questions," or question parts, at the end of the prompt.
5.   **Use key pieces of text.** Make a list of the key sections of actual text, from beginning to end in the work, that address each part of the question. That's all t he outline you need.

Choosing Your Topic

Here, again, is what you need to start any paper, any writing at all. Literally, right now, write down a list of responses to the following. Don't think about them; write them down. Now.

1. A particular piece of text to write about—any specific event, moment, thing. But not an idea, it's got to be an event, a line, an image.
2. The way you see that text, event, or thing—your interpretation, your argument as to why you're bringing it up in the first place.

Starting a paper is as straightforward as these two points. But before you write out your list, here are two things to keep in mind:

First, **beware of sweeping generalizations**. Don't write down generalizations/ideas/non-things as your list items. You're aiming for very specific, exact moments, or events, or lines. Actual *things*, not ideas.

Second, **this step should be done fast**, as it relies on your internal writer's inspiration, your intuition. Nothing kills a piece of writing— before it even gets going—like overthinking. If you're sitting there staring at a blank screen for this step, you're doing it wrong. Just write it, not with your head but with your guts. What occurs to you as you write is what you innately "get." Don't think, write.

Also, when dealing with a lengthy text, like a novel, it's by far easier and more efficacious in the long run if you march through the book from beginning to end.

Both of these assigned forms—the open and the specific prompt—aim toward one end in all of academia: rather than the answers, your classes want you to be able to form the questions. Sure, thermodynamics says that for every action there is an equal and opposite reaction. But why? That's what a paper is all about: articulating the question and figuring out ways to approach it. Every "answer" is arguable. Take that mindset into your paper. Ask. Be open. Be curious.

Let's start from scratch with some examples.

Example 1: *The Great Gatsby*

You've been given an assignment to write an open-topic paper about *The Great Gatsby*. You already addressed Step 1 (your voice) and Step 2 (intention to show with evidence). Next, for Step 3, you'll look for that one specific piece of text that will focus your paper by quickly writing down some lines and scenes that come to mind as you think back on the novel. Here's what you write down:

a) The first dinner party scene: "I have a nice place here," says Tom.

b) Gatsby's first party that Nick goes to (Prohibition? Parties?): "I hear he's a bootlegger," says a guest.

c) The Gatsby-meets-Daisy-again scene at Nick's house in the rain – the clock nearly falls off the mantel; the "counterfeit ease" line in this scene.

d) The scene at the hotel (look up facts on Plaza Hotel?), "He wanted her to say that she never loved him."

Example 2: Social Studies Class

Now, let's switch it up and say you are given an open-topic paper on the Cuban Missile Crisis, here is what your list might look like:

Cuban Missile Crisis:

a)   Sept 4, 1962 - Kennedy public warning

b)   Kennedy brothers' Oval Office meeting(s), early October

c)   Kennedy's letter to Khrushchev, Oct 22

d)   Oct 26, ABC News go-between offer by Soviets

Or if you were a given a multiple-part prompt on the U.S. entrance into World War I, you might write down the following:

U.S. Entrance into WWI:

a)   November 28, 1912 – It's public that Germany will stand by Austria.

b)   December – Wilhelm basically calling British "idiots"

c)   Wilhelm's relationship with Admiral Muller in 1912-13

d)   January 1914, French Poincare dinner at German embassy in Paris

Notice the details in these two lists for history papers: they might have come from class lectures, but they may also have come from an enterprising student doing a little research on the Internet to fill in the gaps in both the reading and lecture.

Research Your Topic to Get Started

A quick note here on the miracle of the Internet. Whenever you're given anything at all to explain, you have to make yourself an expert on that topic. That's what your instructors do themselves. Often, before class, those instructors of yours will be looking up a quick fact or two on what they're about to present. You should think about doing the same thing before choosing one of those specific pieces of text you wrote down for this paper you're conceiving.

Here are a few Internet search guidelines:

1. You're looking for facts. So if you type in "Great Gatsby" into the search bar, you'll come up with Spark, Shmoop, and pages of cheat sites. The best you can find on such pages is plot summaries and generalizations (and often misinform-ation)—the death of your writing intuition.

2. Instead, type in "1920 American culture," or "F. Scott Fitzgerald," or "prohibition," or even American materialism." The idea is to follow your hunches about those lines you wrote down.

3. Wikipedia is usually OK for quick research, but "edu" sites are invariably more complete and detailed.

TAKE BREAKS EVERY HOUR

You have to take breaks during the writing process. People who write for a living generally give themselves at least a few days between drafts, if not weeks. The reason for these breaks is to

1. Let ideas percolate in your non-editing brain, and
2. Step outside yourself and see your thinking and writing from a third-person argument-of-view.

You're thinking, *Nice concept, but I've only got one night to write this paper!*

Most teachers get this, but they still grade papers as if you took days to write the thing. Perhaps you will be given time to draft and redraft as part of an ongoing assignment, but the cruel fact is that most high school and college students have to bang out a paper in a weekend or one tension-filled, energy-drink fueled Wild Night.

Even if you only have two hours to do the whole thing—ouch—you still have to take some breaks, even if it's just ten minutes of working on something else. Best, of course, is to go get some more coffee with a friend so you can keep stressing out together.

Step 4:
Find Your Argument -
The Point You'll Make

Ok, you took a little break and now you're back, and—hopefully—somewhat recharged and can see your jottings with fresh eyes. You've got several specific events or lines of text written out on paper. Now you have to determine if the lines that you selected are, as we say, "writeable." In other words, do they open up a discussion of questions contained in the book / article / poem / textbook? You already know that you can't generalize or write in clichés, but similarly, the point you make cannot just be a "shut-down"—a conclusive statement with nowhere to go but what is said. How to find a line that opens up discussion in this book? You'll have to **think analytically**.

Thinking Analytically

Analysis is the breaking down of a whole into its component parts to see how each part contributes to and creates the whole. You see that book you're supposed to be writing about? Each line of text is in there for a good reason; your job is to figure out why. That line in front of you now, or that moment that sticks out in your mind—it's important. But why? Could the writer have left it out and produced the same effect? Obviously not. So *why not*?

To figure out the significance of each element of a text, and what effect each produces in helping make the whole (the whole effect of the work), ask yourself the three analytical questions, over and over.

The Three Analytical Questions

1. Why is this happening (in the book/poem/etc.)?

2. How come? (Why should we care? What's the purpose?)

3. What's the (book's/poem's) point?

Each of the three questions is required, but the third question is the most important: what point is the text making by including this line? Could this piece of text be removed from the book and it'd still be the same book/poem/article? What argument is the text making here? What is our takeaway from our understanding of that piece of text? What does the text mean to our own experience? How does the text impact our past and future?

Every reader of anything you write, no matter what the context— school, business, law, medicine—any field you can think of—is asking "Why? How come?" You get diagnosed with a bad disease, you may well ask your doctor, "Really? Why do you think this? How did this happen?" That doctor will either produce evidence or she will not.

So take the line that you think is meaningful to the book as a whole and ask those questions: Why is this happening? Why is it in here? What is the argument that the text is making with this specific line?

Example 1: The Great Gatsby

Let's take a look at that list you created:

a) The first dinner party scene: "I have a nice place here," says Tom.

b) Gatsby's first party that Nick goes to (Prohibition? Parties?) – "I hear he's a bootlegger," says a guest.

c) The Gatsby-meets-Daisy-again scene at Nick's house in the rain – the clock nearly falls off the mantel; the "counterfeit ease" line in this scene

d) The scene at the hotel (look up facts on Plaza Hotel?); "He wanted her to say that she never loved him."

Now, let's think analytically about each of these moments and lines.

Scene A: The first dinner party scene: "I have a nice place here," says Tom.

1. **Why is this happening?** The declaration by Tom shows he's arrogant and has no way of seeing from another perspective other than his own.

2. **Why should we care?** This incident makes clear that this dinner party scene is both "intimate" and very much not so. This tells us a lot about Tom's character, which is important to everything that happens in this book.

3. **What's the point?** The guests are all playing roles; they are never themselves. (Daisy even says this when she says that she hopes her daughter will only grow up to be a "pretty fool.")

Scene B: Gatsby's first party that Nick goes to (Prohibition? Parties?) – "I hear he's a bootlegger," says a guest.

1. **Why is this happening?** The first party is all about being seen: who's who, and what gossip does someone have to gain more self-importance (note the two girls in yellow dresses who try to put Jordan down; note also Jordan's last put-down—the pose extraordinaire: "You've dyed your hair since then.")

2. **Why should we care?** This kind of socializing (or not) is what's important to this generation.

3. **What's the point?** It's all posing! It's people not being themselves at any cost.

Scene C: The Gatsby-meets-Daisy-again scene at Nick's house in the rain: the clock nearly falls off the mantel; the "counterfeit ease" line in this scene.

1.   **Why is this happening?** Gatsby is trying to be so suave, reclining against the mantelpiece, hands in pockets (a forced look of disinterest), trying to look bored.
2.   **Why should we care?** Here is a complete role that Gatsby has created for himself, a pose.
3.   **What's the point?** Gatsby, who "gives his name to this book," is the ultimate poser, the height of affectedness.

Scene D: The scene at the hotel (look up facts on the now defunct Plaza Hotel?), "He wanted her to say that she never loved him."

1.   **Why is this happening?** Why the Plaza? Why here for this climax? Looking up some things on the now-defunct Plaza Hotel at the south end of Central Park, you learn that if the action of the novel is going to get down to who is the ultimate power-figure in this novel, then it's going to get down to the new money/old money question by placing the climax at the very bastion of old money, The Plaza.
2.   **Why should we care?** Here, Gatsby can't possibly win. He's an affect—a self-created persona—and old money is the ability to be affected without seeming so, or even realizing that it is doing so. Old money must, paradoxically, be entirely unconscious of itself while at the same time lording it.
3.   **What's the point?** Gatsby, a "counterfeit," will never comprehend these people, and Daisy is the be-all and end-all of old money. She is old money itself.

By this process you find yourself drawn to certain arguments more than others. You ask yourself, Where's the connecting argument? Where is the pattern? What significance is there in this pattern? There's an argument here in this puzzle and I can figure this out if I keep asking why these moments HAVE to be in this book. There's a common denominator between parts of texts; find that commonality in the evidence.

There are a hundred "right" interpretations, but you begin to see a common denominator: money—old and new—and how it produces "the pose." It really all comes down to that line you like a lot, "counterfeit ease"—when Gatsby is trying to be so suave in front of his long-lost girlfriend, Daisy. You like that line; it's going to be the core of your essay.

So many scenes in the novel focus on the problem of "real" human contact, versus phoniness. Each scene involves some kind of "counterfeit" behavior. But the reunion scene—the one that ends with Daisy crying into Gatsby's pressed shirts—that's the great one.

Now ask yourself "How? Why? Why is this scene the most meaningful to me?"

Then you realize—and remember that "realizing" things is the gateway to getting this paper off the ground—that Gatsby's "counterfeit ease" in this scene tells you something about the rest of the characters: Tom, Daisy, and Jordan.

And then you suddenly realize, that if you explain that one line, "counterfeit ease," you'll be explaining the whole argument of the book. You've begun to answer the third analytical question: "What is the book's argument?"

Example 2: Social Studies Class

Let's jump back to that social studies class assignment on the Cuban Missile Crisis.

Cuban Missile Crisis:

    a) Sept 4, 1962 - Kennedy public warning

    b) Kennedy brothers' oval office meeting(s), early Oct.

    c) Kennedy's letter to Khrushchev, Oct 22

    d) Oct 26, ABC News go-between offer by Soviets

As you begin to think analytically about these moments, asking and answering the 3 questions, you realize that there was that one line of General Carter's in the Oct. 16 meeting with Kennedy that sticks out: "We have been observing an unusual facility." Was that the key moment in the decision to go forward? You have to remember that there is always debate amongst historians as to which moment is the key moment, and that each can be argued and supported. You must choose one, and you choose this moment. Just as with the Gatsby clock-on-mantel scene, this represents not only a focal point, but an ongoing common denominator in this historical series of events.

Getting Your Thinking off the Ground: *The Great Gatsby*

So, after your realizations, you now have a sense of your topic. Next, brainstorm a sequence of thinking for your paper. Do it fast, two minutes or less. Do it from your gut and not your head. Stick to the line you like ("counterfeit ease"); focus on that line. Here are the several points you get down:

a) Re-meeting Daisy at Nick's house.

b) Everything in Gatsby's life has come down to this.

c) It's over before it starts; he doesn't have a chance. It's all "counterfeit."

d) This seems to say something about the hopes and dreams of the age. Is it an age of self-destructive promise?

e) Conclusion to be drawn: the 1920s were incurably optimistic—us, too?

f) It's always for us, and it was for them, "One fine morning"— blind hope.

g) We're left with wondering whether this dreaming—this "counterfeit"— is preferable to reality. Conclusion: dream is what we do best.

Note that the reasoning here works outward from a specific argument in the book to a set of conclusions about human nature. An essay must connect, from the get-go, to the reader's experience. Any good story you tell does this—it connects. And we can all connect to the "tomorrow's another day" mindset.

The Outline

What you're probably expecting to do next is to create an outline— that pre-writing document that every student hates (and that most professional writers don't use). Good news: what you just wrote, your basic thought process, is basically the same thing as an outline. You just wrote down the key places in the book where "counterfeit ease" shows up as a main concept. And you went from textually specific to saying something about the world we live in. That list we made on Gatsby immediately above is plenty good to get going on the first draft.

As far as outlines are concerned, they're good for speeches and lectures, and for papers where you have been given exacting instructions on organization. But for most articles and papers that rely on the writer discovering important ideas—being inspired—during the process, then elaborate outlines may only stultify a writer's creative sense. If an outline helps you to organize your thoughts and stay on track, then do it. But be sure it doesn't stop your creative momentum. So, it may well be preferable to skip the outline step and just get to writing the draft. The idea is to write—just write—and not freeze yourself with any thinking about "what the teacher wants."

Step 5:
Write the First Draft

Yes, there are going to be drafts, wearisome as that sounds. If you're so under the gun that you have to get this thing done in one swoop, so be it, but it won't be what anyone can consider strong writing. At the very least, plan on a "rough draft," and then a combing-over of that draft to try to catch missing or superfluous elements. But in the reality of strong writing, the final draft ought to have evolved and morphed from the first; it should be a changed and changing document, and not just a copy with some grammatical editing.

A quick note on "rough" and "final" drafts: For the pros, the final draft comes only when the deadline is finally up; there's always something more that can be done to a piece of writing. A dozen drafts is nothing out of the ordinary. The book you're now reading, for example, went through at least ten drafts. So if you're serious, plan for this evolution to happen by starting your papers a week or two in advance.

Momentum First, Design Later
Ok, to get going on the first draft, recall that "argument" you came up with in the last step. It's still undefined in your mind, and you've been told forever that you need to define it and outline it before you start writing. Throw out that notion that you need a perfectly formed idea before you can begin writing; that will only lead to writer's block. What you've got so far is a rough idea. You have not "figured it out," but you do have a "not-bad" direction in which to start writing. Once this next step is finished—the rough draft—you'll be able to move to a clearer, cleaner sense of the overall design.
For now, you can't let yourself worry about the "direction" you're

taking. You've just got to get down the raw material, and yes, it will be raw and much of it will be writing you won't use in the end. Sorry.

It is a truism that we only come to really know things when we either 1) have to teach them, or 2) write about them. This is what your first draft is about: finding out about your thinking and about what you're writing about.

SO JUST GET WRITING. You did some research and made some notes on that list of scenes/lines; you know different ways to think about the word "counterfeit"; and you have consciously, and on scrap paper, written down for yourself how you're going to work with the third analytical question (what's the book's point?). You're ready to go, and here's just one last gut check from Part Three, above, and it's what makes or breaks any writing:

Tell the Truth!

Have some enthusiasm and commitment in what you're putting down. You have to care about what you're saying. You have to *want* or *need* to say it. Great writers are passionate; they don't just slog through their assignments.

What did you really think, and why, and what was the book's argument, in your view? It's always about the third analytical question. What do you *really*, *honestly* think this book's point is in this particular piece of text? Just say it; you can always remove it later if you think you're off base.

Having psyched yourself up to be in your own voice and to really care about this paper, assign yourself a time-period (forty-five minutes is recommended) and write as fast as you can for that amount of time. This draft's purpose is (only) to get every thought in your head down onto the paper. You will shape and edit later. For now, write with your guts. The guidelines for doing so are as follows:

- **DO NOT OUTLINE.**
- **DO NOT STOP TO THINK.**
- **WRITE DOWN WHATEVER IT IS THAT IS IN YOUR HEAD AT THAT SECOND.**
- **TRUST YOURSELF AND WHATEVER COMES TO MIND.**
- **WRITE DOWN EVEN THE THINGS YOU HAVE NO IDEA ABOUT.**
- **DO NOT EDIT, STOP, MUSE, OR OTHERWISE STOP MOVING YOUR FINGERS.**
- **DO NOT STOP. PERIOD.**

Have that list of scenes, plus the ideas you scribbled down, next to you. Just start with the Daisy-rain scene and bang out everything that comes to you. The way to get this going is to begin with, and stay focused on, the **six journalistic questions**:

1. Who ?
2. What?
3. When?
4. Where?
5. How?
6. Why?

Think about any piece of writing you've admired and you'll see that the questions got answered immediately and in depth. Detail it out: show us with evidence and action—these six questions. Remember, too, that while working on the later drafts you can always look up related materials—facts and commentary—on the web, bringing in as much thinking as you can to build upon this first take. But for right now, just keep push the "Why?" and the "What's really up here?"

As you start in on the questions, don't worry about editing or proofreading or grammar or anything related to "rightness." Whatever mistakes you make, that's ok; you can correct them later. Your only job right now is to get down every single thought you have, relevant or not, as pertains to the two sets of questions—journalistic ones first, analytical ones second.

It's a fact of the creative brain that ideas come to us by intuition—not by analyzing or editing ourselves. It's a lot like when we can't remember a name or an idea, but then it comes to us later when we're not thinking about it. That's what has to happen now, so trust your unconscious mind!

The only rule here is to stick to the text—not the overall, general ideas and themes. Write what the instructor can *see*. Write the things themselves, the facts, the evidence from which your argument will naturally emerge. Just follow the trail that the facts present. Follow the trail.

The Facts, Ma'am, and Only the Facts

The rule "Show; don't tell" has always been around for a reason: we only relate to what we can conceptualize, and telling your instructor about an idea is far inferior to showing them some blood-and-guts action.

Theory and concepts—no; things and action in the world of the text—yes.

As you write like Fury herself, like you're being chased by wild dogs, do not sit for over twenty seconds without writing something down. Do not cross out; do not hesitate; do not beat yourself up; and whatever you do, don't stop writing until the time (e.g., the recommended 45 minutes) is up. Three quarters of an hour should yield about 400-500 words, sometimes as high as 800 if you're going all out, just writing. If you come in below 400 words, you're over-analyzing and/or editing too much.

Yes, you're going to throw a lot of this out! But if you don't get it ALL down, there's no way to get to the good stuff. Real writers chuck out way more than 50% of what they initially write.

Next, take a fifteen-minute break, or a much longer one (hours, days) if you have that luxury. During this break, you have to do something totally unrelated (e.g., not for school), and preferably something enjoyable. Air out the few brain cells you've got left. Go for a walk, play badminton, buy your friend a coffee—anything! The only rule is that it's a break—from schoolwork *and* from technology.

After the break, repeat this cycle until you have more material down on paper than you need—ideally a good 50% more than the word- or page-count you've been assigned.

Keep Asking Why

Toward the end of your writing, or maybe even by the middle, you will begin to see connections as you keep asking yourself *why* questions. Keep asking, "Why is this in the book? Why is this important?" Somewhere in the middle, or maybe near the end, of your writing of the first draft, you will begin to see new connections. You will begin to see parts of the story (or poem or article) in a new way. Challenge yourself! Do you really believe that cliché you just wrote down? Don't let yourself off the hook and begin to lapse into a description/summary of the plot. Keep asking why/how each particular moment, each connection, is necessary for understanding the whole work.

That third analytical question is always where you're headed. Consider where these ideas *could* be headed, and go with those directions that suddenly appear. Go with your gut.

By the end of the draft, it's true that, in most cases, you will have no idea what you wrote down. Don't worry if the topic has gotten completely away from you, or if it's "bad" writing, or if it doesn't fulfill the prompt that you've been given. "Trust thyself," said Emerson, the great American philosopher and writer.

Always reward yourself at this point with **another no-tech break**.

Step 6:
Sort It Out

In this step, you begin the process of turning chaos into form. You'll be shaping that raw material into a beginning, middle, and end, and you'll be making sure that what you wrote in the first draft actually does make sense.

At this point, some of you are saying that you're done—that you're just going to look over what's in this one draft and then turn it in. This is the way most students write their papers, and this book won't lecture or shame you. However, if you're right up against the wall on this deadline, you still have to sort out, sequentially, what you just wrote down. The next step, the critique, should only take you about five minutes per page.

The Critique

In this self-critique, it is imperative that you not judge the writing, and that you especially don't judge yourself. **Stay objective.** Also, grammar is not a concern right now; that kind of tinkering comes in the last steps.

The main idea of this critique is to check over the preceding steps of this writing process. Print out a copy of the steps so you can see it at all times; don't try to switch between windows on your screen. This starting a whole new document will help you get that distance and objectivity you need to be able to see what has to stay and what has to go.

First, review the draft—that wandering, digressing mass of words that seems formless right now—using the following steps as a guide. **Stick with this sequence**: move from the beginning to the end.

1. **Check your voice.** Is it you? Is it jargon that contains every huge, overblown, and undefined word known to mankind? Is it littered with "commonplaces," those huge concepts—like "history" and "love" and "suffering"—that don't really mean anything?

2. **Did you show that you've read?** Can the reader tell that you read the material? This means, yet again, the facts, the evidence, the actual *things* of the text—not the unattached ideas.

3. **Did you stick to the facts?** Can the reader move through the paper without having to write "Huh?" in the margins next to every paragraph? Again, it's the facts, the evidence, the examples—and only the facts.

4. **Check for filler and padding.** Are there quotations you don't need? Are there lines that you just added to take up space?

5. **Check for obvious cuts.** At least some of what you wrote is going to be flat-out painful to see on actual paper. Which parts obviously have to go? Which parts are clearly unrelated? Strike through these sections. Do not be afraid of cutting whole paragraphs in a single stroke.

6. **Check for new ideas.** Is there evidence that comes to you now that hasn't yet been included? Maybe references or facts that just came to you? Jot them down in the margins if you printed your draft or make notes on a sheet of paper.

7. **Find the holes.** In every paper, we need to make "concessions"—acknowledgements that there are some worthwhile arguments on the other side of the argument.

Find those concession-insertions as you read through. Get in other people's shoes and read from their critical perspective. Ask of your statements, "Really? Can I get away with saying that?" Where do you need more evidence, and where do you need to concede arguments? Acknowledge and reply to those good points that are counter to your argument.

8. **Check the flow.** Write numbers down next to the points you made, so that you make sure that you're following a sequence in your thinking. Maybe you began with an argument that really needs to come later in the paper, and maybe the end is where you need to start. Look at the paper as a set of sequential numbers.

In most cases, a writer will have to put down many pages just to find her starting argument. One of the most common notes a teacher will leave on a student's paper is "Start here!" Very often, we'll see the ideal starting argument at the very end of what a student has turned in. Look for this "start" as you number your progressive parts, and especially look for that "start" near your end.

Remember, more than anything else, you have to identify the one argument you want to make—your answer to the third analytical question. This answer is probably still a little vague or unclear at this stage. That's ok! Your main job in this whole step is just to figure out "What point is this specific piece of text making?"

So to finish this sorting, you must identify the following:

1. The specific piece of text that is the focus of your analysis.
2. The method/text/sequence of ideas that you see yourself using to answer the third analytical question: "What's the book's point?"

Step 7:
Rewrite The Draft

Get your head in the right place to finish off this essay by reminding yourself of these four concepts that you need for any final draft:

1. HONESTY – You being you, with a sense of humor and some enthusiasm; not you being a getting-through-the-assignment robot.
2. THIRD ANALYTICAL QUESTION – "What's the book's point?" You're going to keep after this like a dog on a bone.
3. FACTS – You're going to make sure that you're only and always analyzing the facts.
4. ALWAYS ASK WHY – You're not going to take anything at face value or by assumption. You're going to explain, show, justify, and put down examples for everything you say. Be skeptical: be asking, "Really? Is this for real!?"

Take your marked-up, hard-copy essay and, in a very general way, maybe with just three big boxes, identify these three major parts of an essay:

1. INTRODUCTION – The third analytical question applied to a specific piece of text, then defining the terms you're using and where you'll be heading.
2. BODY – Taking the reader through your analysis, *showing* copious examples of your thinking.
3. CONCLUSION – Adding up what you've said and "drawing a conclusion," not just summarizing.

You must see your one answer to the third analytical question in all three sections. If not, then head back to the previous step, "Sorting it Out."

Below you'll find the steps for the rewrite of the draft. You ought to be starting a completely new (as in, blank) document, not making revisions to your last draft. Now just follow these steps; stay focused on the sequence and development/support of your reasoning.

Introduction – The First Paragraph

Looking at your "introduction," you have two choices for where you put your thesis—the book/article's point, as you see it. You can include your thesis in the first sentence of your paper, or in the last sentence of the introduction. You have been trained, most likely, to put down some broad introductory statements in the first sentences and then move towards a specific statement at the end of the paragraph. That's perfectly fine, but do beware those huge, clichéd and too obvious first sentences that don't mean anything.

The easiest, clearest, and most powerful way to begin any humanities essay is with that major thesis statement of yours in the very first sentence. To do so, try beginning your essay with the word "when." That way, you launch the paper immediately into evidence, and evidence is what you need to show that you've read and that you've paid attention.

Example 1: *The Great Gatsby*

Let's assume you stuck to that list of scenes in *Gatsby*, above, and that you've written several pages of a first draft on the idea. Those pages are the guts of your thinking.

Using the suggestion above, let's take a look at an example of a first sentence for this paper on *The Great Gatsby*:

> When Jay Gatsby walks into the reunion with Daisy at Nick's house, the reader can clearly see what this novel is about: a man of "counterfeit ease" who is determined to create a "great" life that can never be anything more than a fiction.

It's not beautiful, flowy prose, but it's effective. Here's what we did in that first sentence:

1. We started with "When."
2. We identified the specific text we want the reader to see.
3. We addressed the third analytical question.
4. We were as brief and direct as possible.

As mentioned above, you have two choices. If you do prefer that alternate model for the introduction—general idea first, and then thesis—make sure you are not generalizing with a mean-nothing sentence for the above topic like, "All people want to revisit the past." There's cliché, and then there's specific; choose the latter.

Example 2: Social Studies

For the social studies example we've discussed back in Step 3, you'd start with an incident, as in the interesting line by General Carter about what they thought they saw in Cuba, and then immediately and in the same sentence, state why, according to the facts, that incident is so important and interpretive—"the book's point." History teacher Luis Terrazas says that this argument should be "a bold claim."

Here's an example of an opening for the Cuban Missile Crisis paper:

> When General Carter brought up what couldn't have been conclusive evidence as to missiles in Cuba, he single-handedly and very nearly initiated the destruction of the planet.

That would certainly qualify as bold, and it would also qualify as reasonable, given the evidence in the tapes from the Kennedy meetings.

So now you've clearly stated your main argument in the first sentence of the paper. What do you for the remainder of this first paragraph? With three or so sentences, you should a) define your terms and phrases, and b) explain more of the third analytical question, including where you're headed next.

Example 1: The Great Gatsby

Back to the Gatsby example, here's how the first paragraph takes shape:

> When Jay Gatsby walks into the reunion with Daisy at Nick's house, the reader sees, for the first time, what this novel is about: a man of "counterfeit ease" who is determined to create a "great" life that can never be anything more than a fiction. This scene's unreal-life concept extends beyond Gatsby himself to both Daisy and Nick, as well, and then on from there to Tom and Jordan. It's a painfully awkward scene

that produces its effect by having money and emotion collide head-on in an emotional way that's as gruesome as Myrtle's end. These people can't talk about feelings without running for their wallets, and their individual crashes make perfect metaphoric sense.

1. The first sentence contains, a) the specific text you'll be focusing on, and b) your argument.
2. The middle section of the paragraph develops and defines concepts in the text you cited.
3. The last sentence considers the evidence so far and sets the direction the essay will take.

So, to lay out your first paragraph,

1. Start with "When."
2. Use a phrase (not a whole sentence) from the text.
3. Complete the first sentence with what you will argue is the book's argument—your "claim."
4. In the next sentences, elaborate and define the major terms you used.
5. In the last sentence, make it clear that by looking at this one piece of text, a reader can understand the whole book— maybe even beyond the whole—showing the instructor that you're analyzing, not just describing.

Example 2: Social Studies

Here's a rephrasing of the list above for your social studies paper:

1. Move from the "When" statement to the problem that was created by the event.

2. In the following sentences, identify the historical consequences of the problem.

3. Conclude the introduction with an explanation of the historical significance of this moment.

So, to recap: the simplest way to conceive of that introduction to your essay:

1. In the first sentence, reference a specific piece of text.

2. Ask/answer/interpret that third analytical question: What's the book's point? If you're talking about that specific piece of text, then you're automatically saying something important about the whole book/poem/article.

This method works for anything you'll ever write—humanities, social sciences, business, law, you name it.

The "Body" of the Essay

Ok, you sorted the huge lump of material in the first draft and created a solid introduction, probably one paragraph, maybe two, in which you included a specific piece of text, you addressed the third analytical question, and you included a few sentences explaining and defining key terms and/or concepts. From here, the bulk of your work will be laying out, in sequence, the facts that support your answer of the third analytical question.

But first, there are two critical rules:

Rule #1 - No Formal Outlines!

This bears repeating: you did not create a formal outline earlier, and you will not create one now. You always hated that part anyway, right? And for good reason: it was a huge turn-off that killed your motivation to write.

If in Step 5 you did, in fact, write furiously with your gut and your instinct and your never-ending questions ("why? why? why?"), then you should have plenty of great, though perhaps unorganized, material with which to work. Do not be intimidated by seeming disorganization! Your original outline is still present in that writing; all you will be doing is unearthing that structure. You do not need to create any more of an "outline" than this.

Rule #2 - Tell the Truth!

Make a personal connection with what you're saying! Show your instructor something he may not have considered! Take some risks!

If you go into this draft knowing that you're going to say what you want to say—what you feel you HAVE to say—then the sequencing/outlining will become automatic, just the way it is when you tell a story to your friends at lunch. Do you bring an outline to the coffee shop so that you can argue a point with your friends?

The body of your essay is all about explaining what you just said in those first sentences—your introduction. Exactly as in a conversation with a living person, you will lay out the evidence and then analyze that evidence. This is not plot summary or description; rather, this is a sequencing of the parts of your argument—the facts—that make up the whole of your argument.

Sequencing Ideas

1. Small to big, and
2. Beginning to end

Do not reverse those orders!

Here's a real-life example and a quiz. Read the problem below and arrange the responses that follow in the most appropriate order, thinking about small/big and beginning/end:

Your friend calls you a liar because he heard that you were with his girlfriend and you had told him that you were with your father at a water polo match. While being pinned to the ground, you say that,

a) You revere the concept of friendship and would never lie.

b) You can dial up your father and put him on the phone if he'll get off your chest.

c) The guy from whom he heard this nasty rumor is a cheat and a liar himself, having just last week been caught and pilloried for plagiarizing an English paper.

Your goal here (as I'm sure you're well aware) is to convince your friend that he has made a grievous mistake and, if possible, to make him feel ashamed for even having considered it, and that maybe he should not hurt you badly. So what is the most effective sequence of responses to accomplish this? Certainly not the sequence listed above. It has to be small to big; most factual to most conceptual.

The answer, you will probably agree, is b > c > a.

Sequencing of facts and evidence is *everything*. Present the facts in a logical and natural way—as they come to you. As people often say: the facts should explain themselves. Stop seeing your paper as three things—intro, body, conclusion—and start seeing it as just one argument that you want to make, from beginning to logical end, using sequential evidence.

Example 1: The Great Gatsby

Let's take the Gatsby essay and write out the sequence in that first draft (that should now be in hard copy, all marked up). We're going from beginning to end.

> First, Nick goes to a dinner party. The three people there are completely "counterfeit" and phony. Maybe Nick makes it four. This is a small detail at the beginning of the book.
>
> Second, the next facts come chronologically later and they become more encompassing: the parties on Gatsby's lawn

where no one knows anyone else and where people only care about being seen with the right "crowd."

And third, the "party" is definitely over at the end of the book, both the kind that happens at the mansion, as well as the one that happens for a whole 1920s culture—maybe our own, too.

With these three parts, we've gone, small to big, first to last. The last, you always want to have coincide with the biggest, most encompassing. Here, it's "counterfeit" first on a small, local scale, and then at the end of the paper it's a falsified and corrupt age. You can do that.

It's just one fact after another, each becoming more meaningful to the whole book—the book's argument, the third analytical question. In sequence, we have moved to a universality, a wideness, beginning with specific facts.

Evidence, Facts, Examples, Action:
As you follow a sequence of a point you make to your friends in that coffee shop, you want to stick with all things visual and full of things *happening*, not general ideas, concepts, or subjective opinions; stick with the facts. Show who the players are and what's behind the scenes you've read. It's people and their actions that make up great writing, not disassociated ideas and concepts. We want to see, as in the Gatsby paper, cars driving into ditches, insults at drunken parties, yellow dresses, and the last conversation between Nick and Jordan where things really get weird and awkward.

If it's another social science, there are still stories to tell. The dreadful textbooks you've been made to read are the ones without things going on—no stories, no action. History writer David

McCullough shows how it may be done in his book on the American Revolution, *1776*:

> "As during the escape from Brooklyn, Washington's other daring river-crossing by night, a northeaster was again, decisively, a blessing and a curse—a blessing in that it covered the noise of the crossing, a curse in that, with the ice on the river, it was badly slowing progress when time was of the essence" (274).

Ultimately, we like to read what we can see—action!—and what we like to see most of all is what writers call "trouble." On this evening's TV news, how much time is taken up with cute-zoo-animal stories? Your reader isn't going to stick with you unless you can show, with the six journalistic questions, some real dirt. So weed out the generalizing and get down to showing us the expanse of snow-covered ice sheeting the Potomac.

Quotations:
Do not throw long quotes around; they just get in the way of you telling us about the scouts in the middle of the night clambering up the frozen mud of the river's banks. When you do quote, use words and phrases that will embellish what you can say in your voice. And remember whatever you quote, you need to discuss, explain, and integrate into your sequence. How many quotes do you need? Only as many as will spritz up the evidential feel of your own writing—the power of your own voice. Don't rely on others for what you can do more powerfully yourself.

Paragraph transitions:
Begin working into the main part of the paper by transitioning from the first to successive paragraphs. Every paragraph needs a transition; it takes off from the last one. To create the easiest and clearest paragraph transition, take a word or phrase from the last

sentence of a paragraph and repeat that word or phrase in the first sentence of the next one. If you go with just an idea that crosses between paragraphs, you stand the risk of offending your grader. No transitions = no essay.

How to get into this "body" of your essay? Again, small/big in the beginning to end sequence. What's the most important small piece of evidence with which you should start?

The writing into this new document—this second draft— is probably going to be about 50% new writing and 50% importing from your earlier work. If you find yourself doing nothing but fiddling with existing text, you're wasting your time. What you want to be doing is looking backwards while writing your way forward through the first draft: you're looking to see if each point and its explanation evolves naturally from the last one(s). Be asking yourself, "Is what I'm writing following my previous line of thinking? Am I explaining what I mean? Most competent student writers can state an idea well, but then they just drop it and move on. You have to explain and exemplify what you just claimed.

The Conclusion

Time to bring it to a close. What you should have now is,

1. A statement at the top of your paper in which you have a piece of specific text and an applied and answered third analytical question.

2. A sequence of paragraphs that detail your evidence—the facts of the matter— along with explanations and much "Here's why this is important."

What most students have been taught about the next step in working with the rough draft—the "conclusion"—is to restate the thesis and sum up what they've said. That's fine if your instructor has specifically asked for this form; it's an easy way to complete the paper. However, in real-world writing—journalism, for example—and in most of your humanities papers, the reader wants to see a student "draw a conclusion"—looking at the foregoing analysis and seeing where one can go from here.

Here's how to do it: Treating the body of the essay like an arithmetic problem, add up the evidence and what you've said about the evidence.

Example 1: The Great Gatsby

1. Gatsby's "counterfeit ease" was, in the beginning, shown as his personal problem

2. By the middle, we see that there is a general party mentality for the five major characters that is nothing but fakery.

3. By the end, we see not only Gatsby's house as a "colossal failure," but the whole culture of the New York rich is phony and now "empty" in the last pages.

Sum of that arithmetic (in logic, called "induction"):

4. This personal and spiritual void might extend to us, too, as a universal human tendency.

Remember this: anything you are taught in any course is for the express reason of showing you what you are as a human being— science, English, history, you name it. "Is this book's conclusion— its 'argument'—the same for culture as a whole? What's up?" This learning about ourselves is where every single course you ever take is going. Put that in your paper.

In its simplest form, the effective conclusion always asks, "Where do we end up after all of this evidence?" In other words, make your closing paragraph relevant to the reader.

Here's an example of a conclusion for the short Gatsby essay we've been working on, beginning in the next-to-last paragraph:

> If we look at Nick's friends, the ones who have created so much drama and so much "counterfeit" emotion, we see that Nick has been, as Jordan Baker has called him, "a careless driver." He's not only been just as artificial and unreal as the other characters, but it may be that he's actually elicited all of the bad behavior. Why? Because Nick has been covering up, like we all do, by pointing out the faults of others in the face of his own "dead dream."
>
> The reader sees, maybe more clearly than Nick, that we're always busy dreaming about what our lives could be— skipping over our faults—and the fiction never stops. Nick thinks that, by going back to the Mid-west, the lies will stop, but if we look again at the first pages, we see that the lies were always there and that there may be no end to them. Maybe

with a little honest facing up to our pasts, we wouldn't be "borne back-wards" with Nick into years of regret.

The last sentence is arguably the most important one of the whole essay. It's the one your instructor will have ringing in her ears as she determines your grade. Note that it brings the material to the reader; the sentence comes into our world. Here, you want to be fully in your own voice and as relevant as you can to what's happening to us, outside the book or historical event. This is the place where you get the parting shot, the chance to get us your final message. *Carpe diem.*

Consider aiming for a last phrasing that begins, roughly, "What we finally come to see in the novel, given _____ (and _____), is _____." The key is to make sure that your reader has experienced what you are now saying.

And one more thing: make that last sentence short. Political speechwriters aim for fewer than ten words for a closing sentence— **the shorter the better.**

Step 8:
Check It Over

The hard work is done! Now put in a little more time to check it over. Follow these five steps, in order. Don't perform these checks haphazardly! Do note that the lists are redundant in certain areas, just so you can make sure you got it all right.

Conceptual Check (revising)
Style Check (editing)
Grammar Check (editing)
Mechanics (proofreading)
Final Phrasing Check (editing and proofreading)

You may find that you don't quite understand some of the points below. That's OK, but know that they're important in college writing. These checklist items are easy look-ups in any reference manual, or on an "edu" college writing site that you can find in a minute.

A note on terminology: "editing" is improving both diction (word choice) and syntax (word order); "proofreading" is just checking for spelling, typing, and the errant phrasing mistake.

The most important editing tool you have is your voice. Read your material out loud. If you edit silently, you will pick up nothing.

WRITE OUT LOUD, READ OUT LOUD, EDIT OUT LOUD.

Conceptual Check

Here, you're looking at the big picture. Print out your final draft, and follow these steps, **in order**, and mark the problems with your pen as you READ OUT LOUD, slowly and carefully.

- You can hear your own voice in the paper.

- You showed that you had read all the material by working only in facts.

- There are no huge generalizations or commonplaces.

- There is a specific piece of text in the first line of your paper.

- You answered the third analytical question in either the first or last sentence of the first paragraph, preferably the first.

- There is a clear transition between each paragraph, including between the first two.

- Each paragraph is between three to nine sentences.

- Each paragraph explains a clear fact, example, or piece of evidence.

- Don't wait for your instructor to write, "Why is this important?" or, "Vague" in the margin.

- The evidence is arranged small to big, and beginning to end.

- The conclusion leads to an argument relevant to the reader's own experience.

Style Check

- Style is the WAY in which you are expressing yourself. Look at how the elements in your paper are presented—how the sense and clarity is going to come off to your reader.

- Can a reader easily pick out your thesis—that "book's argument" that you're interpreting?

- Are your paragraphs between 3-9 sentences? Don't write in brutally long paragraphs. Five sentences is a great length.

- Are there transitions between paragraphs, including between your intro and body, and between body and conclusion? The easiest and clearest way to create a transition is to use a word or phrase from the last sentence of a paragraph and then re-use it in the first sentence of the next one.

- Are there any major breaks in thought? Sometimes, you will actually want that break in thought; if so, use a space break to indicate that you're embarking on a new direction. On the other hand, mistaken breaks in thought will occur when a writer sits and thinks without typing anything. Find where you thought too long and then look carefully at those sections for idea-sequencing gaps and skips.

- Look at your quotations. Try not to use lengthy quotes, as your reader will just skip those parts. It's clearest to quote only words and phrases. That way, you'll not only be adding book evidence, but spritzing up your phrasing, as well. And remember, any reader can tell when a student is just inserting quotes to pad and lengthen a paper.

- Don't paraphrase without citing. Generally, the rule is, *There's no such thing as paraphrasing*. Either you're crediting someone with an idea—explaining that person—or you're plagiarizing. Always name your sources.

- Have you padded the essay in any section? That would include a) quotes that are too long, b) plot summary and description, and c) huge generalizations where it's obvious you don't know what you're talking about but trying to seem as though you do, just trying to get "enough to say."

- When you use a quotation, you must first introduce it and then, afterwards, analyze it.

- Are there any brutally long sentences that are impossible for a reader to get through? Vary the length of your sentences.

- Remember, clarity and ease of reading makes for a happy instructor reading experience.

- Learn and memorize the great Rule 17 from Strunk and White's *The Elements of Style*, arguably the summa of all writing books: "Omit needless words." Look how short that rule is. In your editing of your paper, your approach should be, "slash and burn." Try to cut out 50% of your essay; your grader will thank you.

- Does the conclusion stand on its own merit, or does it just repeat what you've already said? Even in the "restatement of thesis" model for which many of your classes will ask, the section should still be seen as a "closing argument": your last chance to convince the jury of how they ought to interpret the evidence before them. The conclusion must connect to the reader—bring him in and include his experience. Make it relevant.

- Consider, as lawyers do in closing arguments, adding some force to that last sentence. Even better, make it short: fewer than ten words is often what speech writers aim for.

Quoting - A quick note and two examples—A "No" and a "Yes"

Do not write…
> On page 16, when Daisy says that she "hopes [her daughter] will be a fool…a beautiful little fool," the book shows her unhappiness (21).

What scene was this from? Locate the text in the book/article/poem. You need to give your reader some context:.

So do write…
> At that very first dinner party at Daisy's, Nick realizes how hopeless is his distant cousin not only in her little sarcasms at dinner, but especially when she "hopes [her daughter] will be a fool…a beautiful little fool" (21).

The first example tells, the second shows. Now, it's on to discussing and analyzing that quote weaving it into your overall point. Here, if your paper is going to be about this "lost" group of people, continue after the quotation to explain the importance of this moment: Daisy is telling Nick how ignorance would be such bliss for a woman in this social world of hers—that she'd very much like to just turn off her brain.

Bottom line: you have to analyze every word you quote, every moment of text that you bring up. Quotes don't explain themselves.

Grammar Check

At the end of the day, grammar matters. It matters a lot. If you don't know some of these rules, look them up or be brave enough to ask your instructor.

- Run-on sentences are what will sink you faster than any other grammar error. Look up both "fused sentences" and "comma splices."

- Run-ons happen very frequently when students are imbedding quotations in their sentences. Beware.

- Sentence fragments have their place in clear writing, but a misuse of one is glaring.

- Put things next to what they modify. The longer your sentence, the more likely it will be that words will lose their attachments to others; the more words, the more difficulty with clarity and grammar. Don't end up with a sentence that says the opposite of what you mean. How to fix? Read everything out loud, carefully. Never begin a quotation after an end mark. Introduce all quotations. Are the commas and end marks in the right places? For instance, most (not all) of your commas and end marks go inside the quotation marks in the United States.

- What tense should you be writing in? Present tense for fiction, past tense for history.

- Try not to use pronouns that do not have clear referents. Beginning a sentence with *This* is never a good idea. Basically, pronouns get you in trouble. Better to be clunky and clear than arty and vague.

- In science, the passive voice is often used; however, to make your prose come alive in the humanities, stay away from the passive. "Use the active voice" (Rule 14, *Elements of Style). [note in that last sentence the position of quote marks and period]

- Don't use parentheses. Readers just skip what you wrote there.

- Practice using dashes; they can add force to your sentence.

- Should that have been a period or a semicolon?

- And something that drives graders insane: the use of "their" instead of "his" or "her." We do it all the time when we speak, e.g., "Every single person has to remember their book tomorrow when they come to class." Wrong. Pay attention to singular-plural combinations.

Mechanical Check

Is your paper MLA, APA, Chicago or whatever format is required by the class? Make sure you know the class-required format:

> Paper formatting:
> Student information
> Title
> Margins
> Spacing
> Font type and size
> In-text citations
> Works Cited and other citation pages

- An easy way to check formatting is to use a sample essay in Part Two of this book as your reference guide. Just make your paper look like these papers.

- Each of your instructors will have her own formatting guidelines, probably given to you in a handout at the beginning of the course. You can look up "MLA Guidelines" on about a hundred internet sites. If you get this part wrong, your instructor will quickly assume that you've been living under a rock.

- Is your title intelligible? An easy formula for title is thesis plus name of work.

- Are your quotation-citations in proper format for the style required by the class?
If a quote takes up over three lines of your paper, you should indent and set off the quotation so that it may be easily read by an instructor. But generally, if you start quoting at length, your reader will do what you'd do—skip all of it. How much will that help you?

- Set up your "Works Cited" pages perfectly. There is no reason for any errors, as you can look up any citation problem you have in the reference manual assigned for that class. If you don't know, ask the instructor. College professors are especially prickly on citation pages. If you have no reference manual, and no directions, go to an "edu" college writing site and you'll find a "How to Cite" page.

- Spell check your paper, then read it over to see if the check didn't pick up erroneously spelled words. A bad spelling mistake early on will pretty much kill your paper.

- Any typos? Also a kill.

- Line spacing: On your computer, choose "no spacing," not "normal." If there is a space break between your paragraphs, it means, technically, that there's a break in thought. You probably don't want that.

- Paginate as per the class requirements.

- If the course includes handouts from which you'll be quoting, ask your instructor before paper-time for his requested citation method. Many teachers differ in what they want to see in a handout-citation.

- Never assume anything when it comes to college formatting. The look of your paper may seem like a small thing to you, but the little things do matter. Read whatever handout you were given as relates to mechanics, or read the syllabus—most of your questions can likely be answered there.

- And before you finish checking over your paper, know that the first way we instructors see your paper is by how neat, organized, and clean-looking it is. It does not start well when a grader picks up a paper that has a spelling error in the title.

Final Phrasing Check

One last time, make yourself read your paper out loud, enunciating every phrase. Go slowly.

- Look to see where you can combine sentences—where you can turn three sentences into one.

- This combine-sentences rule is predicated on the most famous writing rule of all time: Strunk and White's Rule #17: "Omit needless words." We discussed this in the Style Check. Do this relentlessly.

- Read out loud for any remaining clichés—broadly undefined phrases that have been used so many times that they are meaningless. If you're unsure of what a cliché is, then you're definitely using them and your writing is definitely not what it might be.

- Illegal words and phrases: *very, a lot, basically, hopefully, sort of, seems, deals with, it can be said that, it may be argued that, I would argue that, the fact that, is because,* and any other uses of slang that end up only as cliché or that veer towards subjectivity.

- Know your audience. Are you sure that this particular instructor will understand/appreciate, for instance, that last sentence, the one where you make yourself sound like an expert on the universe in general?

- Remember that the reason that you have been taught all of these writing rules is so that you can break them. But break rules on purpose, not by mistake. Break them when it benefits your reader—when you can show you know what you're doing with style, clarity, and enthusiasm. And enthusiasm in writing counts for everything.

CONGRATULATIONS!

If you followed these eight steps, you have survived—possibly—a Wild Night. Of course you're thinking, "Man that was fun! I'd like to read more about these desperately exciting topics!" Well, enthusiastic academic, read on into Part 2: 10 Student Models to see Part One in action.

Part Two
10 Student Models

Introduction
Ten Student Models

Part One of this book showed you how to write the essay, from start to finish, for any class, any level, any venue—any writing you ever have to do, period.

Your first job in any paper is showing that you have read and analyzed the text, and that means presenting evidence. It means sticking to what your reader can see and verify. The following essays show that it's all about the evidence.

Your task is not to invent the wheel and figure out from scratch how to put together an essay; rather, you have only to model your writing on a piece you find in this section. Whatever you do, in and out of school, you need to see examples—models—of activities that are done well. Playing setter for your first time on the volleyball team? It would make sense to watch the best women at the position. You need to see how it's done; that's what this section is all about.

The following essays were chosen out of hundreds for their easy-to-follow, systematic, and interesting approaches. Each one uses the basic approach you read in Part One. If you use the appropriate model as your guide for a given assignment, you can't fail to produce a similarly simple, clear, and effective essay.

Remember, the essays in this section aren't just "good" ones; they're exceptionally clear models of what you read in Part One. They are the theory put into plain and simple practice.

From voice to structure, these pieces—each of which went through draft after draft—achieved not only clarity but force of expression. You'll find them covering a range of approaches, from writings on subject, or theme, or tone, to others that fulfill prompts on prose or verse. You shouldn't have a problem finding a model essay that demonstrates the exact kind of writing that you need to produce.

Here are the basic parts of the model essays in this section. You've gone over these elements in Part One:

1. Voice – Your own, not any kind of jargon. Plain, simple, out-loud.

2. Honesty – Caring about what goes down on the page. If they *make* you regurgitate, then so be it, but real writing is about what YOU believe and can support. Take a lower grade if it means selling your soul to do otherwise. There are some bold remarks in these essays—some nice "risks," as teachers call them.

3. Showing that you read – Use of specific evidence always shows that a writer did the work required by the class. But go further: research, bring in more detail, more explanation.

4. Text – The focus on a specific piece of the writing, an exact location in the article, poem, novel, even oral exam or discussion at lunch.

5. Third analytical question – "What's the book's point?" Why, Why, Why?

6. Facts – Ideas come only after facts. Put ideas/generalizations first, and no one knows what you're getting at.

7. Sequencing – Facts emerge and present themselves in a logical progression: first to last, and small to big.

8.   Conclusion – Adding up what you explained in the paper, then adding it all up to see this new place at which you've arrived. By the end of a strong paper, it's about bringing the material and the discussion to the reader's own experience, making it relevant.

You'll see that the following ten essays are clear models of how to get Part One to happen on paper. Remember also to look at models in your textbooks, newspapers, fiction, or even in the magazines at the grocery-store checkout line (every writer's favorite reading).

But whatever you do, if you want to get good...

READ A LOT.

NOTE ON THE ARRANGEMENT OF MODELS

The models in this section are arranged from the easiest to put together to the most challenging. The ones coming first work with subject-topics that show you a clear and safe way to go; the ones coming later up the ante and begin to work with more complexity and abstraction in themes and tones. Think of the earlier essays (1-5) as great pieces, just more basic in their approach than the later ones. Neither end of the spectrum is "better"; it's just that as you gain more skill and sophistication, you'll gravitate to—and be expected to write—the later models (6-10).

To begin looking at how the papers are arranged, remember that all academic writing has to address one or all of the following three devices—subject, theme, and/or tone—arranged from easier to handle to more difficult as you move through Part Two of this book.

SUBJECT

A "subject" is a thing, an object, an event, an action, a person. It's tangible and immediately visual, usually in a time-specific way. You can point at a subject. It's there in front of you. An example would be Gatsby's house.

Because an object, an image, is right before us, it is the safest and easiest to choose for a paper topic. All you have to do is

a)   Name and show it.
b)   Ask the third analytical question about it.

THEME

A "theme" is a repeated element or idea that runs across and through a work. You may understand the concept of theme from the music you listen to: a recurring sound or sequence of notes. In terms of writing, it is a recurring idea. An example would be the theme of wealth in *The Great Gatsby*.

Because theme happens over the course of the work, a writer has to be careful not to generalize or get off track. Nailing down such an idea that keeps repeating itself in different aspects can be difficult. For this reason, it is not as safe a choice for your paper as subject.

TONE

"Tone" is an emotional element in a work of art or criticism. It is the intangible *sense* we get from reading something, watching a movie, or looking at a painting. It's a hard thing to pin down without a good deal of convincing evidence and very specific language. Writing about tone runs the risk of creating a subjective impression, and objectivity is everything in the papers you write.

An example of tone would be the sense of social awkwardness in so many scenes in *The Great Gatsby*. Students may well say of the end of the novel that it is "depressing"—an assessment of tone that would get a "huh?" from a grader. Due to their potentially subjective nature, essays on tone are not included here.

Again, if in doubt and under the gun, always choose subject. It's the safest and clearest way to go. As far as theme and tone are concerned, know that the facts you'll need to include will be more elusive—not absent, just more difficult to bring forward in clear focus.

The Order of the Ten Models

From Simpler-to-Write, to More Complex and Involved

There are five categories into which the essays fall, extending from the devices above. The first few essays demonstrate the use of subject and theme. The later essays use subject in more involved ways. Also, an essay may cross over between categories.

If you're new to analytical essay writing, focus on writing your paper using the first models; if you've had more practice, work toward the "close reading" you'll find in the later ones.

- Essays on Subject: 1, 2
- Essays on Theme: 3, 4
- Essays Based on Secondary Sources: 5, 6, 7, 8
- Essays Based on a Close Reading: 6, 9, 10
- Essays on Verse: 10

The Illusion of the Sword
in *Beowulf*

CATEGORY: Subject

This open-topic essay sticks to the textbook model of the clear essay:

1.   The subject is an actual thing that a reader can see, visually.
2.   The third analytical question is addressed in the very first sentence, which focuses on a specific piece of text.
3.   The writer makes it extra easy on herself by beginning the essay with the word, "When."

An essay on subject always has the advantage of showing the reader an object, character, or event—that one thing on which the paper will focus. All a writer has to do is keep her eye on that one thing from beginning to end.

HONESTY – The writer saw all sorts of real connections between her own thinking and this great poem. She'd read a book by the great coach Phil Jackson, and she was psyched to write about what she'd seen between a poem so old (750 CE) and something so contemporary (coach of the Chicago Bulls during the Jordan years).

VOICE – There is a complete absence of jargon. It's just her plain and simple voice—just what AP and college graders want to see. A writer's job is to make the reader's an easy one; if it's the other way around, then little good may come.

FACTS – The writer goes through the poem, from beginning to end, starting with the smaller arguments and heading to larger. Note that the conclusion moves from the third-person to include the universal "we" at the end of the essay.

Ms. Kelley's essay is replete with great moments from the action of the poem. Things happen: a hero kills monsters, and dragons threaten all of mankind. The rule is, skip the ideas and get to the drama.

3ᴿᴰ ANALYTICAL QUESTION: WHAT'S THE BOOK'S POINT? – From facts proceed the writer's interpretation: Beowulf does not fully understand the weapon he's depended on for so long; he over-values its material qualities, and this "illusion" of his leads to some serious trouble at the end.

SECONDARY SOURCE USE – The line by the great basketball coach, Phil Jackson, is well-placed and relevant to the poem. It's a good fit—relevant. It's not "coming out of nowhere," as many student ideas are prone to do. Make sure there are good connections between your examples; make them obvious and relevant to your reader's own experience.

Ali Kelley
Mr. Homer
Epic Poetry-Sec 3
10/25/06

The Illusion of the Sword in *Beowulf*

When his promised sword fails for the first time as he strikes
Grendel's "tarhag" mother, Beowulf learns that weapons are an
illusion, merely a reflection of one's own confidence that determines
the outcome of the battle. When Beowulf first receives the blessed
blade, Hrunting, from Unferth, he is honored by its glorious record.

Yet when the auspicious weapon fails, Beowulf responds
courageously, discarding the weapon and confidently seeking his
own tool to overcome the monster. As he discovers a new sword,
Beowulf's self-confidence is affirmed as he attacks the beast for a
second time with a new conviction stemming from his ownership of
the new weapon. Finally, Beowulf defeats the monster, not by a
weapon endowed with past victories, but by his own total
determination. When his task is completed, Beowulf's new
"weapon" dissolves into its original state, leaving him with only a
small remembrance of what he achieved and an everlasting wonder
of what will follow. The sudden disintegration of his efforts

demonstrates the perpetual cycle of wonder in the story of Beowulf: in the search for answers, nothing is ever absolute, and a final solution only leads to a new dilemma.

Initially, Unferth bequeaths his ancestral sword, Hrunting, to Beowulf to avoid involvement in the impending battle. Unferth recognizes that he is not fit for such heroism and Beowulf eagerly accepts his offer to prove himself: "With Hrunting I shall gain glory or die" (103). Suddenly bestowed with a new confidence, Beowulf plunges into the mysterious water alone: "After these words, the prince of the Weather-Geats / was impatient to be away and plunged suddenly: / without more ado, he dived into the heaving / depths of the lake" (103). Thus, Beowulf anticipates the outcome of his battle based on the trust of his comrades. But does Beowulf himself really trust the sword?

Ultimately, Hrunting cannot win the battle because Beowulf does not believe in it: "But he soon found / his battle-torch extinguished: the shining blade / refused to bite. It spared her and failed / the man in his need / . . . here at last / the fabulous powers of that heirloom failed" (105). All of Beowulf's confidence in this argument is derived from the apparent successes of this material object, which he does not understand. The weapon was said to have been sacred in Unferth's family: "It had never failed / the hand of anyone who hefted it in battle" (101), yet what does Unferth's ancestry mean to Beowulf? When Hrunting fails, Beowulf realizes he must accept responsibility for his own actions and develop faith in his own individual strength: "Hygelac's kinsman kept thinking about / his name and fame: he never lost heart. / Then, in a fury, he flung his sword away" (107). Beowulf's conscious decision to abandon his only extra aid demonstrates his raw heroism in accepting that glory is totally personal and can only be achieved alone. In addition, his impulsive shedding of weapons shows an active conscience and a commitment to simplicity and acceptance of Phil Jackson's line, "You've got to work with what you've got" (*Sacred Hoops* 100).

When Beowulf discovers a new sword, he is finally ready to enter the battle because he has ownership of his weapon. He found it by his own means and trusts its strength as he trusts his own: "Then he saw a blade that boded well / . . . an ideal weapon, / one that any warrior would envy, / but so huge and heavy of itself / only Beowulf could wield it in a battle" (107). Beowulf's weapon becomes his psyche: it is so great that only he can control it. The sword is not a weapon in the material sense but a mental weapon of overpowering self-confidence that Beowulf uses to defeat the monster. Immediately after fulfilling his task, Beowulf feels a sense of pride in his own accomplishment: "The sword dripped blood, the swordsman was elated" (109). In this sense, Beowulf reaffirms his personal responsibility for his actions by using his inner strength to defeat external powers.

After he overcomes Grendel's mother with his psychological sword, Beowulf returns to a state of wonder as his indomitable sword disappears before him. As the once concrete weapon formed of Beowulf's conscience dissolves into its original state, everything becomes unknown again: "The sword began to wilt into gory icicles, to slather and thaw. It was a wonderful thing, the way it all melted as ice melts when the Father eases the fetters of the frost and unravels the water-ropes" (111). Beowulf's call for help is answered within himself but rapidly vanishes before him, leaving him in a perpetual state of questioning. Why did Hrunting fail me? Why is my only weapon now disintegrating? Where do I go from here? It is as if this weapon, Beowulf's heroic recognition of his self, provided a fleeting moment of clarity. But as ice melts into water, so solutions drip into questions, and we are left in a perpetual state of "if." Beowulf discovers that only by looking inward can he begin to understand the world around him.

Meanwhile, the other end of the sword is aflame, the scrollwork melting and erasing the past. This concept of the fiery hilt chasing a frozen blade can be interpreted to mean that the past is swallowing the future, eliminating any chance of a present and foreshadowing the end of the world. In Beowulf, fire triumphs over ice, but it was the ice that prevailed over evil. Life is never solid as ice but rather fluid like water; only when we look within ourselves are we able to solidify our existence. Otherwise, we change according to our surroundings, never sure of what came before or what will come after, only certain that in the flow of life, "there is no permanence" (*The Epic of Gilgamesh* 106).

Works Cited

Beowulf. Trans. Seamus Heaney. New York: W.W. Norton, 2000.
　　Print.

The Epic of Gilgamesh. Trans. N. K. Sanders. New York: Penguin,
　　1972. Print.

Jackson, Phil, and Hugh Delehanty. *Sacred Hoops: Spiritual Lessons
　　of a Hardwood Warrior.* New York: Hyperion, 1995. Print.

The File in
Great Expectations

CATEGORY: Subject

This open-topic essay is very clear as to the third analytical question: What is the book's point? This writer even uses that phrase in her first sentence—the "the point" that the book is making. For this writer, the message of the whole novel is contained in just one thing—the file that shows up in the very beginning of the novel.

Compare the first sentences in both the *Beowulf* essay and this one: both use the same easy formula—focus on a specific subject/piece of text—that throws the writer into the discussion of the facts of the book.

HONESTY – The writer wants to head to the moral lesson that Dickens gives us in all of his work: we are all equals—"sons and daughters of Adam"—no matter what our pay grade (*Little Dorrit*). Ms. Barnes here makes it clear that she's thought beyond class about this material.

VOICE – No jargon.

SPECIFIC PIECE OF TEXT – The "chains" and the "file" on which she focuses are fully concrete, plain, and visual. She sticks to a simple argument involving the concept of subject.

FACTS – In each presentation of a piece of evidence, the writer considers her argument in varying ways, as in the third paragraph where she shifts perspective to another character than the protagonist, Pip.

3ᴿᴰ ANALYTICAL QUESTION: WHAT'S THE BOOK'S POINT? – The thesis here begins with the idea of "struggle" and ends in the conclusion that brings the message out to us: the answer to Pip's problems—"love."

Kendall Barnes
Ms. Strobridge
Victorian Literature-Sec 7
2/28/02

The File in *Great Expectations*

The file that Pip gives to the convict in the first part of *Great Expectations* is used to make the point that we all are searching for something to free us from our "chains." Throughout the beginning of *Great Expectations*, Pip searches for this "file" that will free him of what he calls the "universal struggle," or life as he knows it. He looks for this facilitator of freedom in the convict, Joe, and Biddy.

Pip does not give the convict the file and food out of fear. He helps the convict because he sees himself mirrored in the poor and disheveled man, and by helping him, Pip feels that perhaps, he can help himself. Pip identifies with the convict in numerous ways. Both are alone in the suffocating environment of Victorian England. The convict, freshly escaped from the Hulks, is uncannily similar to Pip, who has briefly run away from his own prison, his home. We see Pip perhaps even feeling sorry for the convict: "I looked over my shoulder, and saw him going on again towards the river, still hugging himself in both arms, and picking his way with his sore feet" (7). Here, Pip acknowledges the convict's pain, rather than ignoring it, showing his pity for the man. His pity establishes a relationship between him and the convict which, as we see later through the convict's false confession, borders on affectionate. Pip, while afraid of the convict, also possesses a desire to help the man, because he sees so much of himself in him. Perhaps by helping the convict by giving him most importantly the file, Pip can for a brief period be relieved of his own suffering.

It cannot be ignored that the file which Pip gives to "his convict" is Joe's file. Not only does Pip look for relief from his suffering in the convict, but Joe too plays an even larger role in Pip's search for freedom, for it is Joe who, at the beginning of the novel, is the largest "file" in Pip's life. Joe and Pip are regarded at the beginning of the book, essentially, as equals, or more specifically as Pip says, "fellow sufferers" (11). It is because of this equality and Joe's pity that Joe is able to relieve Pip of some of his own suffering. This relief is illustrated in the dinner scene in which Joe is constantly pouring Pip gravy to lighten the heavy conversation taking place at the table, regarding Pip. Joe serves as a sufficient source of alleviation until Pip begins to spend time with Miss Havisham and

Pip is no longer satisfied with Joe's "commonness"; he moves from simple sources of relief, to education—in order to make himself feel not so common—and ultimately away from the goal he doesn't know, Biddy.

While Biddy is able to provide a small amount of remission for Pip, Pip sees his eventual freedom in receiving the love and acceptance of Estella. While "it [is] clear that Biddy [is] immeasurably better than Estella, and the plain honest working life to which [Pip] was born, had nothing in it to be ashamed of" (132), it is at the same time apparent that Pip wishes he could win Estella's love when he says to Biddy, "I wish you could put me right. . . . If I could only get myself to fall in love with you" (131). It is evident here, that Pip's file is not in education, but rather in Estella's acceptance and love.

Work Cited

Dickens, Charles. *Great Expectations*. New York: Penguin, 1996.
    Print.

"Do Good!"
Says "Gooseberries"

Category: Theme

These are the two reasons to read this essay, which was an "open topic" paper on one of Anton Chekhov's short stories: 1) it's plain and simple, and 2) the writer had a moral argument he wanted to make. The writer was a student who was interested in human rights work, and when he read the story, "Gooseberries," he was taken by the urgency of the narrator's call to get off our butts and help others. When you read this essay, you'll see what it means to be engaged, to want to say something that's important, and to say it now.

Honesty – The writer, PJ O'Neil, is fully connected to the message he found in the story: to get readers to work for others. The paper reads almost like a speech, maybe even a sermon. It's enthusiastic.

Voice – It's his own, plain, natural voice, as opposed to an academic one. Simplicity = clarity = an appreciative reader (grader).

Text – The essay couldn't be more direct in focusing the reader's attention on a specific piece of text: "Do good!"

Facts – He takes great lines from the story and explains each one. There are examples and plenty of explanatory support. He does not rely solely on quotes; he explains.

3rd Analytical Question: What's the book's point? – You only have to read the title of the essay to get this message. Note that an effective title contains two elements: thesis and name of work.

Secondary Source Use – The verse from the *New Testament* near the end gives context and support to the analysis.

Conclusion – Without any kind of repetition here, the essay brings the book to us, to our lives. It broadens out into a message, the mark of any strong conclusion.

PJ O'Neil
Prof. Robartes
Russian Lit – Sec 1
10/21/08

"Do Good!" Says "Gooseberries"

Chekhov's "Gooseberries" passionately argues that one must do good without any regard for one's own happiness. Happiness, "Gooseberries" says, is only possible because the dying, the malnourished, and the sick bear their burdens silently. Helping to "bear the crosses" of the weak and the suffering may allow one to transcend happiness and gain "something more intelligent and great." The time is now; while one is still young and capable, one must give up all idleness and conceit to help those silently suffering.

The story wants to make it very clear that happiness is not possible if one can see or even hear the suffering that is happening throughout the world. Conveniently, for the "happy" characters of the story, all the unhappiness has been left behind in the city. Suffering, as characters like Nikolai suggest, is something humans are inclined to ignore. The country place where Nikolai strives to one day live seems like a natural ambition for most. The city is depressing; there are too many bleak people there. It is normal to want to be happy, even if that happiness is a lie because, "dearer to us than a host of truths is an exalting illusion" (317). Human logic tells us that we must ignore the "statistics: so many gone mad, so many buckets drunk, so many children dead of malnutrition" because "obviously the happy man feels good only because the unhappy bear their burden silently. Without that silence happiness would be impossible" (318). Happiness is passive. It doesn't require really living of any sort. The only requirement for happiness, as the story clearly arguments out, is to run away to a country place. Happiness is idle, devoid of spirituality, and so it is unfulfilling.

Perhaps more disturbing than Nikolai's disregard for human life in general is his disregard for his own life. Moving to the country place represents a surrender. Nikolai is no longer interested in living his own life. He is utterly weak: "To leave town, quit the struggle and noise of life, go and hide in your country place, isn't life, it's egoism, laziness, it's a sort of monasticism, but a monasticism without spiritual endeavor" (314). The suffering of people in the city never crosses his mind. He isn't even living his own life, much less worrying about the lives of others. There is no purpose to his existence: "It's a common saying that man needs only six feet of earth. But it's a corpse that needs six feet not man. Man needs the whole earth, the whole of nature, where he can express at liberty all the properties and particularities of his free spirit" (314). Man needs to appreciate his own life before he can face the suffering of others. After one has experienced the preciousness of one's own life, including the struggles and the happy times, the suffering of others isn't an inconvenience anymore. Bearing the crosses of others isn't a burden anymore, it is just a necessity. One is bound to the suffering through the preciousness of life. This is when real spirituality kicks in, but "Gooseberries" has a hard time explaining this phenomenon, so it turns to the Bible, in particular to the story of Jesus' crucifixion.

Jesus' story isn't important because he "died for our sins." It is important because he felt human emotions—he was scared and asked God to have mercy on him, but he still sacrificed himself. His own life became a secondary importance; the collective life of mankind became his first priority. The Bible says: "Each of us should please his neighbor for his good, to build him up. For even Christ did not please himself but, as it is written: 'The insults of those who insult you have fallen on me'" (*Romans* 15:2-3). It is the responsibility of the strong to bear the crosses of the weak. And obviously the Bible does not mean physically strong. It means that the ones who have had the luxury of figuring out how precious life is are responsible for helping others to have the luxury to come to that same realization. This is Nikolai's greatest sin: he had that luxury, but instead he disregarded his own life and forced the weak to carry their own crosses. By the end of the story Ivan is essentially yelling at the reader. While one is young, while the passion for life is still pumping through one's veins, one must do good!

> Don't settle in, don't let yourself fall asleep! As long as you're young, strong, energetic, don't weary of doing good! There is no happiness and there shouldn't be, and if there is any meaning and purpose in life, then that meaning and purpose are not at all in our happiness, but something more intelligent and great. Do good! (319)

"Gooseberries" leaves nothing to the imagination: understand how precious your life is and the concern for the suffering will come and their crosses will weigh nothing.

Works Cited

Chekhov, Anton. *Stories of Anton Chekhov*. Trans. Richard Pevear
    and Larissa Volokhonsky. New York: Modern Library,
    2000. Print.

The NIV Study Bible. Grand Rapids: Zondervan. 2002. Print.

Russian Breath

CATEGORY: Theme

This essay was in response to the prompt, "What theme do you see running across the books you have read in this survey of Russian literature?" While the idea in this paper might at first seem a little extreme, it is a) defined and explained throughout the first paragraph, and then 2) tied to a plethora of evidence beginning in the second paragraph. Note that this evidence is entirely visual and presented in the writer's own detailing of each example; he does not rely on quotations to stand in for his own showing of facts.

The strong first sentence is an attention-grabber; it forces us immediately into agreeing or disagreeing. That's the basis for interpretive analysis. From that first sentence, the theme is developed, expanded, and finally concluded upon in the essay's last textual reference and then in the last paragraph. The essay comes full circle in that last sentence.

HONESTY – The writer is fully connected to what he shows in the essay; he believes strongly in what he's saying. It's clear to a grader that he has read the books very carefully, and very personally. And he <u>cares</u>.

VOICE – That honesty translates into clear, strong voice. We want to read this person. He's a good storyteller; he makes the action come alive for us. The best part about this essay is that Mr. Larner-Lewis does not just drop quotes into the paper and move on; he develops each story with a great deal of power. The depiction of the meal scene in Solzhenitsyn's novel, for example, makes the paper come alive. So forget the quotes; do the work yourself.

SURVEY OF TEXTUAL EXAMPLES – While there is not one specific piece of text on which the essay focuses, each of the examples used in the essay come together in the conclusion, redefining for us the idea in his title, "Russian Breath."

FACTS – Note how the facts sequence themselves, one into the next. He arranges them from the most vivid first—the prison scene—to the most figurative—that poem at the end. There is no forcing in the structure of the essay. The reason? The writer doesn't have to rely on abstract ideas; he just sticks to one key example in each of the books he read.

3RD ANALYTICAL QUESTION: WHAT'S THE BOOK'S POINT? – It's right in the first sentence, then explained in the rest of the paragraph, then shown with examples throughout the essay: Russians have dealt with a lot more than most other cultures, and that has made them see the world as a place of difficulty, not of ease and happiness.

Jon Larner-Lewis
Prof. Mishkin
Russian Literature 312
11/4/99

Russian Breath

Russian literature is about social suffocation. Essentially,

Russians are unable to breathe under the stifling weight of their

history—a history of oppression, suppression, and suffering. Every

great writer from that country has criticized the social climate of his

time. This critical attitude spans a thousand years and exists across

all classes, becoming, in the literature, a sort of self-satire; because,

while it is true that Russia has had its share of tyrannical leaders, it is

the people of Russia who are their own bane. In a country where

there is never enough of anything to go around, social competition,

the need to assert oneself over one's neighbor, is heightened to

dangerous levels.

The clearest example of this cutthroat social structure is

inside the gulag in *One Day in the Life of Ivan Denisovich*. The book

is a realistic portrayal of life in a Stalinist labor camp, but it is also a

microcosm of the Russian condition. This Russia is the biggest forced labor camp in the world. With millions of oppressed citizens fighting each other for scraps under the watchful eyes of a merciless police force, the lines of the barbed wire fences begin to blur and expand. Returning to a camp after a day of work, Ivan thinks, "Who's a zek's [prisoner's] main enemy? Another zek" (119). The "squealers" survive; any small advantage gained helps make life more bearable, even if it is gained at the expense of another. The evening meal scene in Day in the Life is one of the most horrifying and ironic in all of Russian literature. The men fight, cheat, and steal just to get their allotted bowl of thin stew. Ivan literally fights his way through the crowd to get to his squadron and then has to secure a tray by cheating another squad and pushing a man to the floor. Finally, he sits down to his meal, but while he's eating, he has his arms wrapped around the bowl, cautious to the argument of paranoia. Throughout this scene, one forgets that all these men are trying to do is eat after a day of hard labor in subzero temperatures.

One might think this mentality is confined to the camps, but any Russian who was involved in the riots and famines around the Revolution and the Civil War would tell otherwise. One must fight for every gain and guard it with frugal caution.

In Solzhenitsyn's other story of life under Stalin, "An Incident at Krechetovka Station," we learn that the tendency to rat on one's neighbor in order to become more secure is a practice not only of those under the rule of the Party. In order to get ahead, or even just to survive within the ranks, paranoia and back-stabbing must become second nature. Zotov is a Red Army lieutenant working at a train station during World War II. He is a good socialist; he reads Marx and abstains from women. He is cold and efficient in his work, "deep into the matter of rail routings" (43). Yet Zotov is no machine. He is very human, complete with pangs of conscience and pity. When a stranger comes to the station saying he has lost his echelon, Zotov is very taken with him at first. The man is a naïve and friendly actor from Moscow who is dressed eccentrically and has been through a humorous ordeal. But when he makes mistakes in the course of conversation that suggest a poor knowledge of socialism, Zotov becomes suspicious. His trained paranoia ("Be calm. Be vigilant!") leads him to arrest this man whom he had come to like (43). Though the matter is left open, most likely the stranger was not a spy, but merely a poor, distracted actor. Constant suspicion of one's fellow citizens was one of the central, most harmful tools of

Stalinist rule, but Stalin did not invent it; he found it deep within the Russian psyche. Solzhenitsyn shows this universal character flaw exploited by Stalin to ruinous effect.

Social competition does not exist only under Communism or during wartime, as Anton Chekhov, another one of Russia's most acute and caustic social critics, shows us in his brilliant short stories and plays. In "The Dance Pianist," we meet Rublyov, a poor pianist who plays at weddings. While there, he is shamed and embarrassed by the guests for talking to the bride, though she initiated conversation. He grows furious the more he thinks about it until he is thrown out of the party. His crime was in becoming conscious of this handicap in the Russian soul. He tells his roommate, "What is it in the Russian character, I wondered, that makes it possible, as long as you are free . . . to drink with a man, slap him on the belly . . . but as soon as you are in a slightly subordinate relation to him, the shoemaker must stick to his last!" (65) Rublyov realizes that Russians are so class-conscious as to be vicious. The wealthy people take pleasure in ridiculing him, not because of what he has done, but because they are in the social position to do so. Rublyov has been abused because of his low status one too many times, and finally he goes mad. In Solzhenitsyn, being vicious is a means of survival, but in Chekhov's upper classes, viciousness is a pastime.

Before Chekhov, Tolstoy had addressed this pastime in his moral tale, *The Death of Ivan Ilyich*. When Ilyich, a prominent bureaucrat, dies, his colleagues who "had all liked him," immediately being thinking about his death's "possible effect in the way of transfer or promotion for themselves or their associates" (101). Tolstoy goes on to show us the agonizing death of a man whose life had passed him by in a blur of promotions, social functions, and high-stakes card games. Tolstoy, who is big on messages, makes this one very clear: No true peace of mind can be found in the grips of Russian high society. The most educated and successful people in the country are, spiritually, its worst failures.

Tolstoy echoes this message in *Anna Karenina* by using the ill-fated affair of Anna and Vronsky as an example. The couple is doomed from the start because there is no room for true passion in their social sphere. Decadence, diversion, and status reign, and love is one of the many casualties. Karenin will not grant Anna a divorce because it would give him the reputation of weakness, and his reputation is what he values most. This means that the affair will always remain just that—another affair, unworthy of recognition. Even Vronsky feels that he must continue to move in his old social circles, despite his newfound passion. He neglects Anna, and this leads both to her suicide and to the utter dissolution of his life.

It is the artist's job to help people perceive and understand their faults. Good artists are social critics; in Russian literature, this is particularly true. Art aids self-awareness. The social, political, and economic conditions of Russia are so full of conflict, hardship, and suppression, that self-reflection and personal identity suffer; just look at *Crime and Punishment*. Russians of all classes are so used to being oppressed, be it by Tartars, serf-owners, czars, the nobility, or the Party, that they grasp at any form of self-assertion they can. Whether in a bread line or at the whist and billiards tables, these instances of social maneuvering come at the expense of others. The people end up stifled and suffocated by one another.

In a poem called "The Artist," Alexander Blok writes,

> And when at last the conception is imminent—
> New soul, new forces about to draw breath—
> Meteor-like a curse strikes. In a moment
> Artifice chokes inspiration to death. (*Selected Poems* 87)

Most Russians are not afforded the luxury of inspiration, as they are suffocated by the competition brought on by the "artifice" of social situations or by hard necessity. Luckily, the country has a wealth of great artists who are inspired and who illuminate the country's problems and strengths. They urge their countrymen to throw off the stranglehold of Russian social structure and to draw their own, sweet breath.

Works Cited

Blok, Alexander *Selected Poems*. Trans. Jon Stallworthy and Peter France. Manchester: Carcanet, 2000. Print.

Chekhov, Anton. *Selected Stories*. New York: Signet, 1960. Print.

Solzhenitsyn, Alexander. "An Incident at Krechetovka Station." *"We Never Make Mistakes." Two Short Novels*. Trans. Paul W. Blackstock. New York: W. W. Norton & Co., 1963. Print.

Solzhenitsyn, Alexander. *One Day in the Life of Ivan Denisovitch*. New York: Signet, 1963. Print.

Tolstoy, Leo. "The Death of Ivan Ilyich." *"The Death of Ivan Ilyich" and Other Stories*. New York: Penguin, 1960. Print.

The Island in *Adventures of Huckleberry Finn* as an Allegory for Eden

CATEGORY: Subject, Literary Device, and Character Study

To get this essay going, the writer chose a literary device that would define this novel for him. That device, allegory, is the most traditional of all literary frameworks, stretching from the middle ages up into the present day. Using this device, writers have drawn exact parallels between the figures on the page and the ideas they wanted to denote. An example is that famous fifteenth-century play, *Everyman*, in which the title character is simply "every man" among us; he has friends with names like Strength, and Beauty, and Good Deeds. Allegory is pretty easy; it's not symbol, something that needs a lot of interpretation. Here, that argument is that Huck is a new version of the biblical Adam. Huck isn't just like Adam in the novel, says Mr. Ferrugia, he *is* Adam.

VOICE – In this essay, there is a good deal of exacting literary terminology and the writer is a little more formal than in the previous models. There are some technical terms that have to be used, and what he does well is to explain those terms with plain and simple phrasings of examples and explanations. You won't have trouble seeing the good clarity in the essay.

SPECIFIC FOCUS ON ONE SCENE – The writer stays focused on one scene—a specific piece of text—from the novel, taking us through from its beginning to its end. It's a natural and logical sequence that he follows. He does not allow the technical ideas to dictate his movement of thought; instead, it's just his following the facts as they unfold that makes the essay work well.

3RD ANALYTICAL QUESTION: WHAT'S THE BOOK'S POINT? – In the first sentence of the essay, we know exactly what is the writer's point—his argument or thesis, as you hear it called in your classes. From this first sentence, it's just a matter of taking us through the scene, supporting his point on allegory with evidence from both the novel itself and from the *Old Testament*.

SECONDARY SOURCES – From the get-go, the writer refers to the biblical story, and then to his readings in Emerson and Thoreau—the Transcendentalists. The essay, in pursuing the sequence of facts, works to fuse the novel, the Bible, and Twain's romantic philosophy.

CONCLUSION – The last paragraph of the essay does the arithmetic—adds up the preceding paragraphs—and ends with a nice turn: Huck is Adam, and Adam would have done well to have lived in the American Midwest. That's "drawing a conclusion."

Jon Ferrugia
Ms. Duke
American Literature – 4
2/14/03

The Island in *Adventures of Huckleberry Finn* as an Allegory for Eden

"I laid there in the grass and the cool shade, thinking about things and feeling rested and ruther [sic] comfortable and satisfied. . . . A couple of squirrels set on a limb and jabbered at me very friendly" (*Norton Anthology* 1,287).

Samuel Clemens, in *Adventures of Huckleberry Finn*, portrays Jackson's Island as Eden itself and its inhabitant, Huck, as a new and transcendental Adam. Huck is a boy connected with the natural world around him. Adam became master of the Garden of Eden; here, Huck becomes transcendentally connected to his Eden. Guided by his sense of virtue, Huck is content simply to be a part of the island, and his intrinsic relationship with nature allows him to complete Clemens's revisionist allegory in which Adam becomes a transccndcntalist.

The allegory begins with the manner in which Huck arrives on the island. Escaping to Jackson's Island to save himself from his alcoholic, violent Pap, he crosses the Mississippi under the cover of darkness, arriving on the island just before dawn, and decides to "lay down for a nap before breakfast" (Norton 1,287). It is as if he has been reborn in this place, or created in it, like Adam. He finds himself lying undisturbed in soft grass under the trees, with squirrels chattering around him. He is immediately in the midst of this Eden; he is part of it. The connection he feels with the world around him reflects the transcendentalist view of the story, as he is "powerful . . . comfortable" from the moment he wakes up until he leaves the place a few chapters later (1,287).

Despite being "ruther [sic] comfortable and satisfied" in this benevolent natural environment, Huck begins to feel "sort of lonesome" (1,287, 1,289), without anything to appease this loneliness, much as Adam feels the same way in his inability to find "a suitable partner" among the animals (Genesis 2:20). Before long, though, Adam finds Eve, and Huck finds Jim. Certainly, there is not the physical relationship that Adam comes to know, but Jim does dispel Huck's loneliness; Huck is "glad to see him" (1,290). This relationship reflects the intellectual and intrinsic quality of transcendentalism, and moves away from the physical and extrinsic nature of the Bible story. As Huck begins to accept Jim, they begin to learn from one another in their exchange of ideas; here is the move from biblical beliefs to those of the transcendentalists.

Clemens completes the revisionist allegory by establishing Huck's connection with the animals on the island, which are all tamed by a flood. Huck says that "you could paddle right up and put your hand on them if you wanted to" (1,289). This example of the benignity of nature is comparable to the gentle character of Eden's fauna before the Fall. Just as Adam had "dominion over the fish of the sea, the birds of the air, and all living things that move on this earth" (*Gen.* 2:28), Huck is "the boss of [the island]; it all belonged to [him] to say" (1,289). But there is one marked difference between the way Huck rules the island and the way and Adam rules the garden: Huck does not try to "rule" at all. He does attempt to "own" such a wild and benevolent place; he shows this through his reaction to the flood-tamed animals, declaring, "We could have had pets enough if we'd wanted them" (1,289). He clearly has no desire to assume control. He seems to be guided by his inner virtue that allows him to be connected to the natural world without asserting his dominion over it; he is comfortable just "being." This connection, as opposed to "dominion," reflects the Emersonian move that the book makes from external to internal.

Huck is linked to the Edenic environment—is part of it—and so transcends human barriers. He is not restrained by the same social mores that shackle the other characters of his world: He befriends a slave, runs away from his father, and the animals on the island treat him as one of their own. As Huck connects fully to the world around him, the book moves the emphasis from the extrinsic mastery over the animals that Adam exerts to the intrinsic realization that Huck enters into as he awakes on the island. Clemens gives less importance to "doing" and more to "being," and by doing so accentuates a revised spirituality, creating a transcendentalist model for the novels of the future.

Works Cited

Clemens, Samuel. *Adventures of Huckleberry Finn. The Norton Anthology of American Literature*. Ed. Nina Baym, et al. Shorter 5th ed. New York: W.W. Norton, 1999. 1,265–1,453. Print.

The NIV Study Bible. Grand Rapids: Zondervan. 2002. Print.

Gregor's Female Counterpart in Kafka's *The Metamorphosis*

CATEGORY: Subject, Secondary Source

This essay was written as an open-topic assignment in a course on literary modernism. The teacher in that course prized close reading over all other methods of encountering literary texts, and this student got that memo. What began the essay was simply a brainstorming session involving the Why/What/How-come questions: What are the key elements of the story? Of what parts is it made? What things does a reader see? What actions are created as a result of those things?

There are no "right" questions, just all good ones if they aim toward the third question, the one getting at the book's argument.

VOICE – Note the slightly more formal academic language in this paper. There is some "literary" phrasing, but still no diction that qualifies as full-blown jargon. But do note the more university-influenced voice.

TEXT – This essay zeroes in on and nails down a particular thing in Kafka's story: a cut-out picture from a magazine. It doesn't get any more specific than that.

3rd ANALYTICAL QUESTION: WHAT'S THE BOOK'S POINT? – That magazine photo must, the writer figures, play a huge role in the protagonist's process of decay. Why a photo, and why this particular one? How does the magazine fit into and affect the story's action? Ultimately, could this "subject" be removed from the story without adverse effect?

SPECIFIC PIECE OF TEXT – The writer never strays from the magazine, even when looking at actions that come before or after the photo's direct reference.

FACTS – The key element of Mr. Holt's use of facts is his constant questioning of how the parts of the story work. The facts come in a sequence from small to all-encompassing, from the woman in the picture to the real woman outside the magazine, the protagonist's sister. And as with any good presentation of facts, this writer marches through the story from the relevant moment, onward to the conclusion of the story.

SECONDARY SOURCE USE – While the focus is on the magazine photo, the use of a couple of articles in the back of the student's edition of Kafka, written by well-known literary critics, added much credibility to this student's argument. Studying these scholarly essays prior to writing his own, the writer saw a path into considering this particular subject: he had certain agreements with, as well as disagreements with, the interpretation of story-events he read in the articles. This essay, then, is not only a close look at subject, but a reply to those important articles written on *The Metamorphosis*. The point here is, Do some research.

Alex Holt
Mr. Mills
Modernism – Sec. 5
1/17/06

Gregor's Female Counterpart in Kafka's *The Metamorphosis*

In the second paragraph of *The Metamorphosis*, Kafka presents the only character to whom Gregor feels emotionally connected: a model from a magazine cutout. Kafka portrays Gregor as a character whose hopeless disconnection from humanity causes his own family to reject him. The framed magazine cutout that hangs on Gregor's wall serves as a petty exception to this disconnection. Nevertheless, in a story fraught with human loneliness, such a small connection stands as the only sufficient hope for contentment. However, Kafka does not merely express connections between the two. He even goes so far as to establish the lady as Gregor's "soulmate"—not only his love interest but his absolute complement. Kafka makes it clear that the model serves as Gregor's female counterpart through the two characters' shared occupation and fate as well as through Gregor's attachment to her.

Kafka presents the model in such a way that reveals the similarities between her occupation and Gregor's. As Kafka makes us aware that Gregor is a "traveling salesman," the relation between the salesman and model may be quite clear to us as both work as vendors of goods (Corngold 3). Kafka subtly hints further at this similarity by his description of the model as "raising [her product] up against the viewer" (Corngold 3, emphasis mine). With any luck, Corngold's word choice here is at least somewhat accurate and we can safely assume that Kafka intends to depict the model as aggressive in the way that a salesman might be. However, I would warn against going as far as Sokel's idea of drawing the conclusion that the lady exerts hostility (Corngold 66). This unfair accusation bases itself more upon the harshness of the atmosphere than the text itself. Such an accusation withdraws the hope which the picture supplies. Kafka then draws further comparison between the two characters upon the common products which they sell. Before describing the model, Kafka hesitates to remark upon the "unpacked line of fabric samples" spread beneath the magazine cutout, drawing our attention to the items which Gregor sells (Corngold 3). He then continues on to portray the model as donning a "fur hat and a fur boa" as well as holding up a "heavy fur muff" (Corngold 3). The similarity lies in the comparison between the two fabric products.

The wooly muff that Kafka describes draws another association between the two characters; both become consumed by their own livelihood. Before I begin, allow me a bit of a digression. First, we must accept the idea that Corngold's translation may not capture the entire connotation behind each term (it would be ridiculous to assume him, or anyone, capable of such). The term to which I shall refer is the German word (ungeziefer), which Corngold translates as "vermin" (Corngold 3). In its full German context, this term contains undertones of parasitism and belligerence (Corngold 62). Such a freeloading creature and a salesman have much in common in that they both thrive aggressively and dependently off of others; thus, it would not be a mistake to conclude that Gregor has merely become the acute version of his profession. His job has consumed him entirely, disturbing even his body. The beautiful model shares in this awful fate as Kafka describes the heavy fur muff "in which her whole forearm [disappears]" (Corngold 3). The model thus suffers a similar, ironic ailment as Gregor does: her business shall inevitably consume her, while in the case of Gregor, it already has.

Kafka expresses Gregor's severe attachment to his fellow-infate during the scene in which his sister and mother remove items from his room. When Gregor senses a threat toward the cutout, he "hurriedly crawl[s] up on [the framed cutout] and press[es] himself against the glass," protecting it from his family (Corngold 34). Though some may disagree, I have noted this action as the single self-serving event which Gregor takes on in the story's entirety. From the onset of the story until this argument, Gregor has remained completely unselfish in his deeds, working only to help his family and send his sister to a Music Conservatory. Kafka even states that Gregor "would rather fly in Grete's face," than allow her to take the cutout away, going so far as to harm his sister whom he was previously so willing to aid (ibid. 34). Politzer observes that the soothing of Gregor's hot belly by the cool glass of the frame indicates a unity of love between Gregor and the model (Corngold 87). Once again, Sokel's analysis cheapens the power of the text. Though I will admit him correct in discovering the unity, his idea of the relationship is based merely upon love while the truth (if such a term is allowed in fictional analysis) is much more powerful. The frame "soothes Gregor's hot belly" because he has finally achieved contentment through contact with the model—he has been reconnected with his other half (Corngold 34).

By providing Gregor with a significant other, Kafka provides one of the only senses of hope that the novel contains. However, the form that it appears in adds quite sad social commentary to the work. Even though it is quite fortunate that Gregor even has a soul mate, that it comes as a representative of the new manufactured society emphasizes another of Kafka's arguments. Since Gregor took the picture from a magazine, the only true love which Gregor can find has already been mechanized and reproduced thousands of times; therefore, it is not unique.

Works Cited

Kafka, Franz. *The Metamorphosis*. Ed. and transl. Stanley Corngold. New York: Bantam, 1972. Print.

Sokel, Walter. "Education for Tragedy." *The Metamorphosis*. Ed. and transl. Stanley Corngold. New York: Bantam, 1972. 1 60–80. Print.

Ophelia Lives in "Menocide"

Category: Subject (Character), Secondary Source

A writer's passion for, say, heavy metal, head-banging music can be brought to bear on a literary analysis. So could an interest in art history, or physics, or politics be brought to bear on a book in a humanities class. Any secondary source that is of the same ilk as the primary one is a good bet to help you explain the third analytical question. Writers are always thinking in the vein, "Let me give you an example." Or, "If you understand this secondary context, you'll understand the primary one in a whole new light."

Here, the writer imagines Ophelia, from *Hamlet*, in the context of some serious Metal. The image is strong, for sure. A reader could ask, "Is there a real connection between the character in the play and the narrator of this song, 'Menocide'?" The answer is definitely yes. The lesson for writers here is to reach, but to maintain similarity while taking that risk.

Voice – If you know the Metal genre, you'll recognize the barely controlled rage in the language of the writer, Ms. Watson. She's definitely had enough.

Honesty – A writer who's willing to use her own voice—here, the one that won't accept any more of the "male-dominated environment"—already has the reader by the throat when she writes the first sentence.

Facts – The writer just follows the lyric-sequence of the song, from start to finish, bringing in cuts from *Hamlet* to exemplify the song's point, and vice versa.

3RD ANALYTICAL QUESTION – WHAT'S THE BOOK'S POINT? –
This essay uses the time-honored concept of going exactly 180 degrees from what is called in literary studies, "the dominant reading." In other words, she listened to the popular interpretations in class, and then argued the exact other way. Throughout history, Ophelia has been read as a demure, submissive victim—a casualty; here, in the song "Menocide," she gets to tell her side of the story.

Secondary Sources – This entire essay follows along with the lyrics from one song, bringing in the character Ophelia with each new stanza. The writer is continually saying, "If you understand this song, you can understand Ophelia, just in a different way than she's generally been read—as in, polar-opposite different.

You should listen to the song to get the full effect of the essay. The wall of sound is impressive.

Hannah Watson
Mr. Lee
Shakespeare 2032
11/20/04

Ophelia Lives in "Menocide"

Shakespeare's masterpiece *Hamlet* is fraught with tragedy, but the most pitiable character lives on in today's culture. Ophelia, silenced into madness, finally finds a voice in contemporary music. Otep is a heavy metal music group with a strong feminist bent, named after the lead singer and lyricist, Otep Shamaya. The band's song "Menocide," from its CD *Sevas Tra*, represents Ophelia's cry of frustration at living in a smothering environment. The song's narrator and Ophelia are the same woman. Ophelia lives under her family's control; the narrator/singer of "Menocide" is tired of having her life dictated. For both Ophelia and Otep, suicide is a desirable ending because of the deification incurred therein. Ophelia's death is an act of liberation, while the song is a cry to arms of all females living in subjugation.

Ophelia suffers from the very beginning of the play when she allocates her selfhood to her family. After being instructed to beware Hamlet's false love, she promises not to forget Laertes's admonitions: "'Tis in my memory locked, / And you yourself shall keep the key of it" (I.iii.85–6). She willingly gives her brother free access to her mind. Since he is the only one that has "the key of it," she should be strong enough to remain independent even with him inside her head. But then she reveals that she is just as malleable for her father: "I do not know my lord what I should think" (I.iii.104). Ophelia invites Polonius to advise her on love, but his guidance quickly turns to manipulation. And by the time the dialogue with her lover begins in earnest, she has lost herself: "I think nothing my lord," (III.ii.104) she says when he for asks her opinion. Now Hamlet has a means to fill her head with his madness. With all the men in her skull, there is no room left for Ophelia. She has no thought that is not carefully censored by the men around her. She is reduced to a living puppet.

The narrator of "Menocide" does not go as willingly into servitude, but she nevertheless finds herself stifled in a male-dominated environment. The attack of the song is a list of how all the aspects of her life are controlled: "—what to wear—what to eat—what to feel—what to think—how to act—how to speak—insecure—incomplete!! ENOUGH!!!" The narrator's existence is judged based on how well she abides the constrictions of her masters—the clothes she wears, the food she eats, the emotions she feels, et cetera—and rather than be victimized with criticism, she reclaims her life and calls for a rebellion against those who own her.

Ophelia is unable to resist her tormentors—after all, she let them in—but she still manages to make her final (and only) stand at a "weeping brook." Gertrude's famous speech of Act IV, Scene vii alludes to the fact that Ophelia's death is intentional. Gertrude even hints at how she originally intended to kill herself: "There on the pendant boughs her coronet weeds / Clamb'ring to hang" (lines 172–3). Ophelia "clambered" into the tree to hang herself with her "coronet weeds." Naturally, plants thin enough to be twisted together into "fantastic garlands" (l. 168) are too weak to support a limp body, so Ophelia's hanging turns into a drowning when the vines snap. Gertrude only says, "an envious sliver broke" (l. 173); she doesn't mention a willow branch because that isn't what cracks. The spliced strands of Ophelia's "weedy trophies" (l. 174) are what sever. Ophelia's only intention at the river is to escape her life.

The narrator of the Otep song is confronted with life threats on all sides, so her only perceived safety is to take her life before anyone else can. The song opens with, "killing me, he's killing me, we killing me, me killing me, killing me." The only choice she has that remains unaffected by dominant powers is the manner in which she dies. It becomes a ceremony for her, complete with chants and incantations. She intones, "this is the beginning of my Liberation!" like a prayer similar to Ophelia's "melodious lay" (l. 182). Death is therefore a twofold freedom for them: they break the shackles of deportment and at the same time achieve spiritual deliverance.

As sinful as suicide is in the Catholic Church, it is Ophelia's salvation. Her death by water is not "muddy," (l. 183) as Gertrude puts it, but transcendent. The brook is a baptismal font in which Ophelia immerses herself to be completely transfigured. While her clothes absorb the liquid and become "mermaid-like" (l. 176), her body adjusts to the water until she becomes "a creature native and indued / Unto that element" (l. 179–80). Her physical appearance doesn't change, but her spiritual state ascends from the cloistered world of man to the openness and innate splendor of nature. The "weeping brook" is not mournful; its tears are for the joy of her absolution.

The Otep song has a holiness of a different sort, but it is no less sanctifying. The narrator prays to her own goddesses for their blessings: "Lilith, Eve, Isis, Kali. GIVE ME FREE!!" The mantra-style in which she sings reinforces the ritual with which Ophelia commits suicide. The invocation of powerful female deities from many pantheons ensures a complete benediction. The narrator assumes the matriarchal qualities of Celtic Lilith, the maternal love of Christian Eve, the power over the afterlife of Egyptian Isis, and the omnipotence of Hindu Kali. The narrator fulfills her destiny as she calls for rebellion: "no compassion, kill your masters!" Gifted with divine prowess, she calls for an uprising to end the suffering of women and to exterminate tyrannical males across space and time. The narrator rises into eternity alongside some of the most powerful women in mythology.

The oppression, abuse, and insanity of Shakespeare's Ophelia are vindicated in the pounding rhythms and aggressive vocals of Otep's "Menocide." Both women's lives are only worth their obedience. Ophelia and the narrator in "Menocide" are driven to suicide because they have no opportunities to alleviate the bleakness of servitude. Ophelia is nothing more than a vessel for her family's thoughts and desires. The singer of "Menocide" is at the mercy of her masters, but unlike the Shakespearian maid, the singer finds an outlet for her aggravation in music. The voice of the song is much more powerful than Ophelia's due to the passion of expression as opposed to the absolute lack of freedom whatsoever in Ophelia's household. Otep's song "Menocide" is a tribute to women like Ophelia who struggle for freedom and buy it at the cost of their lives.

Works Cited

Shakespeare, William. *Hamlet.* New York: Folger, 2003. Print.

Otep. "Menocide." *Sevas Tra*. Emi-Capitol Entertainment, 2002. Recording.

Hamlet as Holden's Bad Role Model in *The Catcher in the Rye*

CATEGORY: Subject (Character) and Secondary Source

One of the main elements in humanities instruction is thinking in terms of connections—links that don't at first seem as if they will hold together. In this essay, the elements of the preceding models—subject, character, theme—are integrated to create a complex look at a seemingly straight-forward novel by Salinger. What the essay shows us is that analysis is able to make us see that what we had thought was easy is something new, startling, and complex. Who would have thought that a scene at an afternoon play would explain so much about an entire novel, as well about maybe the greatest play ever written? Remember, your instructors <u>want</u> you to identify complexity, even if there are no answers. Questions, more than answers, are the soul of academics.

VOICE – With so much detailed, moment-by-moment analysis, the writer has to choose words that explain clearly. The writer's voice here is plain, simple, direct. Think of the great "Rule 16" in *The Elements of Style*: "Use definite, specific, and concrete language." Jargon tends more often than not to violate this key rule.

SPECIFIC PIECE OF TEXT – In the moment that Holden becomes annoyed with a woman sitting in front of him at Radio City Music Hall, we see a whole novel encapsulated.

FACTS – Every line in this essay is generated by a particular moment in either *Hamlet* or *Catcher in the Rye*. Ms. Wehrle begins immediately with a scene, an action, a fact, and then she continues to dig into and under what makes this moment, analyzing it from the perspective of the Shakespearian refrain she sticks in our heads: "John-a-dreams." Refrains work; use them often.

3RD ANALYTICAL QUESTION – WHAT'S THE BOOK'S POINT? –
Seeing references to Hamlet all over this novel, the writer has only to ask herself, "Why is this play imbedded in this novel to such a great degree? How come? What's the effect, the point?"

SECONDARY SOURCE – The very essay itself is based on a specific piece of text from maybe the most famous play of all time. The question a writer asks herself before any writing is, "What connection can I bring to this topic that will help me explain what this is about?"

Kelly Wehrle
Hampshire College
8/15/06

Hamlet as Holden's Bad Role Model in *The Catcher in the Rye*

In Salinger's *The Catcher in the Rye*, Holden's affinity for

Shakespeare's *Hamlet* deepens when he sits next to the crying

woman at Radio City and starts pretending to be Hamlet. Holden has

shown his interest in Hamlet ever since he began telling the story of

"this madman stuff that happened to me" (1). With "madman,"

Holden references Hamlet's feigned insanity in dealing with the bad

"stuff" happening in Denmark. He actually starts imitating Hamlet at

Radio City by saying "take somebody that cries their goddam eyes

out over phony stuff in the movies, and nine times out of ten they're

mean bastards at heart" (140). This unusual idea comes directly from

Hamlet, who is also baffled by people who weep over fictional

situations. Seeing an actor crying on stage makes him wonder, "Is it

not monstrous that this player here, / But in a fiction . . . Could force

his soul so to [put] tears in his eyes" (2.2.503–508). But Holden

makes Hamlet his role model at Radio City not because he relates to

Hamlet and his troubles, but because he sees him as a hero. Holden needs to play the hero here to cover up the insecurity he feels next to the crying woman. She threatens him because he is incapable of showing emotion towards anything, and this suppressed frustration is what propels Holden aimlessly through New York.

Holden's underlying anxiety comes through in the way he alters Hamlet's original sentiments about the actor. Hamlet is introspective, contrasting himself to the crying player: he says that the player's tears are "monstrous" to him not only because they have no real source, but also because Hamlet can show no emotion towards his own situation (2.2.503). Hamlet should have a lot to be upset about in the days following his father's murder, but he only mopes about "like John-a-dreams" feeling frustrated (2.2.520). The actor's distress makes Hamlet's passiveness more obvious, and he admits it.

Holden, however, attacks the crying woman to distract the reader from his inability to cry, and this cruelty drives him even farther from his heroic vision of Hamlet. The "monstrous" irony that Holden chooses to see is different from Hamlet's irony—he attacks the woman as a monster, calling her a "mean bastard" and a "goddam wolf," instead of attacking himself. By echoing Hamlet, however, Holden inadvertently implies what he refuses to say: that he has the same problem as Hamlet and hates his inability to react to anything as he drifts around New York City, much like "John-a-dreams." But rather than admit his self-disgust, he becomes the "mean bastard," attacking the woman and distorting Hamlet's opinion in a weak attempt to rub his flaws off onto someone else.

Yet Holden does admit to one of his weaknesses, his cowardice, to further ally himself with Hamlet. Holden bemoans his inaction, repeatedly calling himself "yellow" (88), just as Hamlet decides after hearing the player's speech that he must be "a coward" because he has not defied his mother or avenged his father (2.2.523). Holden thinks his fear will draw him closer to Hamlet, but he acts more yellow than Hamlet as he chooses to insult the woman. Further, by calling her a "wolf," Holden's fearful avoidance of his own weaknesses grows clearer. Since wolves are often stereotyped to be brave animals, he elevates the woman's bravery above his own—the woman is braver than Holden because facing one's own emotions, even absurd ones, takes courage. Both Holden and Hamlet would undoubtedly be afraid to cry, especially at a performance, because it would make them appear weak.

Holden takes comfort in Hamlet because he is also a "sad, screwed up type guy" with a habit of self-repression (117). However, when he sees the play *Hamlet* with D.B. and Phoebe, he finds the actor who plays Hamlet is "too much like a goddam general" (117). Seeing Hamlet parade about confidently makes Holden feel even more sad and screwed up in comparison. As he watches Hamlet finally take action and (accidentally) kill Polonius, as well as most of the royal court, Holden can no longer ignore how he lets his own depression fester within him. He does not consider that, perhaps, Hamlet is a bad role model who sets a terrible example in the way he violently reacts to his suffering. It does not even matter that Hamlet's murders lead to his own death: what matters to Holden is that Hamlet breaks free of his thoughts and acts, while Holden gets left behind.

Yet murdering everyone in New York will not help Holden any more than it did Hamlet. Hamlet is a dangerous hero for Holden because he mistakenly assumes it is brave to rashly act on one's emotions, no matter the consequences. Only by ripping himself from Hamlet can Holden deal with the self-doubt that drove him to emulate Hamlet in the first place. He does so when Phoebe rides on the carousel and Holden starts "damn near bawling," finally breaking through his emotional barrier without murdering anyone (213). Like the woman's tears, Holden's lack a clear purpose: he says he is crying out of happiness, but "[doesn't] know why" he is so happy (213). When Holden lets down his defenses and gives up on Hamlet's "heroism," he is able to weep—something Hamlet was never brave enough to do.

Hamlet continues to suffer because he never sheds a tear: he offers to "weep" over Ophelia, and insists that "I'll do't," but here Hamlet uses his tears only as a way to compete with Laertes's grief (5.1.242–4). Hamlet can only weep if he can "do't" like an action, because he still believes crying is weak unless the tears have a calculated purpose. Holden's ability to disagree with Hamlet and weep with sincerity saves him from Hamlet's fate of being eternally stuck in a melodramatic daydream—that is, of becoming a real "John-a-dreams."

Works Cited

Salinger, J. D. *The Catcher in the Rye*. Boston: Little, Brown, 1991. Print.

Shakespeare, William. *Hamlet*. Cambridge: Cambridge University Press, 2005. Print.

Where in New York City is Holden Caulfield?: The Use of Simile in *The Catcher in the Rye*

CATEGORY: Close Reading

VOICE – There's no jargon here, even though the tendency would be to include a great deal, as there is some sophisticated theory in both the thesis and in its explication. What the writer is able to pull off is a clarification of how language is used in Salinger's novel, on both a surface and then an underlying figurative level. What Ms. Kelley was able to do was to draw conclusions from some very easy facts involving suitcases, breakfasts, and insane mother. The main thing to note is how the essay steps from evidence to conclusions.

CLOSE READING - "Close reading" is a prying into the individual words in a text and seeing what kinds of meanings those words yield. Close reading is the summa of academic writing, where a writer explores words not as general concepts, but as specific "referents" that may mean different things in different contexts—punning, for example. Here, the writer looks at language using the principle of referential meaning: simile, where one word is likened to another—one concept to another to show meaning in original ways.

SPECIFIC PIECE OF TEXT – Close reading is always based on a specific piece of text, a place in the writing where meaning is hinged—where the book or article pivots. Here, it's in a scene involving two suitcases and two nuns. The essay just keeps asking itself questions as to what these scenes are doing in the novel—why they <u>have</u> to be there.

FACTS – The principle behind close reading is the fact on the page: what really are the suitcases in this essay's interpretation? Are they just bags, or are they connotations of what is happening in the character's head? Why suitcases and not, say, baskets or shopping bags? It's always the "Why?"

3RD ANALYTICAL QUESTION – WHAT'S THE BOOK'S POINT? – From the basic "Why?" questions, the main task for a writer is to ask, "Why is this section in the text? What argument does it make? Could it be taken out? If so, would it be the same book?"

SEQUENCE – The writer, noting the use of simile in her scene, starts and follows a discussion of simile to where it leads—the inside of Holden Caulfield's thinking. Look at her topic sentences: they're guides for the sequence. Sequence is always 1) first to last, and 2) small to big.

CONCLUSION - In this essay, the concluding paragraph adds up the evidence from each paragraph and then arrives at the conclusion that Holden Caulfield is "split apart," given the way he expresses himself in schisms, in splits between himself and world. So, the conclusion has to lead to the question, "Do we try and join with our worlds, or do we work against ourselves to splinter experience?" It seems that it isn't a rhetorical question; i.e., human beings maybe tend naturally toward self-destructive thinking and behavior. Now there's an argument to be taken up.

Lindsay Kelley
Brown University
Summer, 2000

Where in New York City Is Holden Caulfield?:
The Use of Simile in *The Catcher in the Rye*

In the middle of J. D. Salinger's *The Catcher in the Rye*,

Holden Caulfield stores his bags in Grand Central Station and eats

breakfast with two nuns, who are also traveling with luggage. After

observing the nuns' "very inexpensive-looking suitcases," Holden

revisits Elkton Hills and Dick Slagle, confessing that although "it

sounds terrible to say . . . I can even get to hate somebody, just

looking at them, if they have cheap suitcases with them" (108).

Before leaving the sandwich shop, Holden recalls the Whooton

School and Louis Shaney, whose memory rekindles his fear "that

[the nuns would] all of a sudden try to find out if I was Catholic"

(112). Holden connects the second monologue to the first using

simile: "It's just like those suitcases I was telling you about, in a

way" (113). Unlike metaphor, which declares that one thing is

another, simile likens one thing to another; joining words create

potentially complicated spaces between the two things being

compared. In the breakfast scene, simile does not describe a union of two things or ideas; instead, the gap created by joining words allows Holden to escape himself and other people, fracturing and silencing the connections he longs to make.

Salinger uses simile in several ways, sometimes very casually, and sometimes more seriously. While wondering what a nun must think about when reading "certain books," Holden does not just wonder; he wonders "like a bastard" (110). Holden avoids saying that he is a bastard; instead, this phrase defines a feeling that is typical, common, banal, but also taboo: desire. Later in the scene, Holden apologizes for accidentally blowing smoke in the nuns' direction. He apologizes "like a madman," but does not say that he is a madman (113). Holden's psychological state has little to do with his decision to apologize for blowing the smoke. The phrase "like a madman" is similar to "like a bastard"; both describe emotional terrain that is familiar and poignant—in this case, the feeling of shame that leads to a profuse apology. "Like a madman" and "like a bastard" surface several times in the novel, and may be interpreted differently each time, but in the breakfast scene, these phrases illustrate Holden's preference for casual, indirect transmission of difficult subject matter.

Halfway through the scene, Holden remarks that "the one with glasses . . . reminded me a little bit of old Ernest Morrow's mother, the one I met on the train. When she smiled, mostly" (112). With the phrase "reminded me a little bit," the comparison becomes simile, creating a gap between the two women. This simile is different from "like a bastard" and "like a madman" because the space created by the joining words is defined. Adding the fragment "When she smiled, mostly" creates a memory. Holden sees the smile of the nun and the smile of Ernest Morrow's mother simultaneously, but backs away from direct comparison; after all, his subjective, first-person memory is the only connection between the two. Simile shields Holden from direct comparisons, but also involves him: Holden himself is the thread connecting one to the other one, the joining word: "like."

When Holden concludes, "It's just like those suitcases I was telling you about, in a way" (113), Salinger creates one of the largest, most fertile gaps in the novel. Just as Holden fills the gap between the teacher and the mother with a smile, he fills this gap with an equally tenuous connection, "nice conversation": "It's just like those suitcases I was telling you about, in a way. All I'm saying is that it's no good for a nice conversation. That's all I'm saying" (113). The relationship between Dick Slagle, the nuns and their suitcases, and Louis Shaney is complicated, but not unreadable. Although issues of class and religion are pertinent to Holden's struggle to articulate himself, what distinguishes this comparison from others in the scene is only partially the weight of the discourses involved.

Simile gives Holden a characteristically vague and slippery means of escaping his own desire, shame, and complexity. While attempting to describe "nice conversation" and opening up a space between his two interior monologues, Holden stops short, not defining "it" while qualifying "it" with the statement, "That's all I'm saying" (113). At this stage of *The Catcher in the Rye*, simile opens up gaps but also provides a structure for shutting down direct communication. Simile fractures Holden's voice into many voices; amid the cacophony of these competing voices, he can barely speak at all. Where there might have been a jumping-off argument—"nice conversation"—there is instead self-censorship and qualification— "That's all I'm saying." Simile, then, splits Holden apart. The device suggests, in its gaps and with its joining of words, a course that might bring him back together again, but simile does not allow

Holden the direct, tangible language that would enable immediate

connection and reconstruction.

Work Cited

Salinger, J. D. *The Catcher in the Rye*. Boston: Little, Brown, 1991.
    Print.

The Resetting of the Cycle in
"The Second Coming"

CATEGORY: Close Reading

"Close reading" is the goal of all academic reading. You saw it in the last several essays, above. The easiest way to get into this task is to choose one specific place in the text and explain that one spot as a representative moment in the whole thing. In a piece of verse, such as in this great poem by William Butler Yeats, the start-point is the word "gyre." What Ms. Ramos will do is to define this term, then walk through the poem, beginning to end, asking herself why this word is the crux—focal point—behind the meaning of the poem.

THE STEPS:

1.   Choose a key word or phrase that appears to be 1) meaningful in itself, and 2) a motivating idea for the larger meaning of the work.

2.   Apply the third analytical question to this one word or phrase and decide on an interpretation of that word or phrase.

3.   Start your essay as any other: steps 1 and 2 in the same first sentence.

4.   Begin walking through the poem, line by line, section by section, showing how that key word or phrase is creating the meaning for the poem.

5.   Arrive at the end of the poem showing how that word or phrase has turned—means more and other than what it did in the beginning; all great verse makes us see something

much differently at the end, than we had at the beginning. You must show that transformation of the original concept in the conclusion to your paper.

VOICE – Writing about verse is all about diction (word choice) and syntax (word order). It's a close look at how each word means a) something on its own, and b) something that makes a whole. So be careful of that jargon, and while you're at it, try not to use too many pronouns or adjectives, both of which can lead to ambiguity.

SEQUENCE – Writing about verse is easy in this regard: start at the beginning and just march through the thing. Don't skip any parts and don't write about a line or section out of its sequence as you see it on the page. Going for a huge idea that is not sequential is never a good idea in any writing, no matter if it's prose or verse or email or that love letter you have in mind.

3ᴿᴰ ANALYTICAL QUESTION – WHAT'S THE BOOK'S POINT? – Make it arguable. Many who read this essay will not agree with Ms. Ramos' conclusion, and that's what you want. If you're just writing plot summary or generalization, you're not making it in the "critical thinking" department.

CONCLUSION – In every piece of great verse, there is some sort of "turn" at the end, as writers call it. It's your job as a critic to evaluate how that transformation works. You're only being given great literature, so there must be something dramatic happening, especially in the ends of these poems. What is it and how do you interpret it? And lastly, you must—absolutely must—bring it to the reader's experience. In this essay, the conclusion pushes the reader to consider a spiritual, personal reading of the poem.

DRAFTING – This essay, like the other nine in this section, took at least a half-dozen drafts to become "ready for prime time," as it were, and it should be noted that these are good writers who labored like Sisyphus over these papers. This writer worked on at least ten drafts. Most of her work during the editing process centered on the following basic parts of the essay, in this order:

1.   Sequencing of evidence: putting the facts in order.
2.   Major points/arguments and their location in the essay: addressing the third question.
3.   Explanations (showing) of those arguments: explaining both facts and the writer's points.

In your first drafts, you'll find yourself jumbled up and wandering in your sequencing—totally expected in the evolution of an essay. Editing is where a second pair of (trained) eyes can really help. Warning: do not give the paper to your roommate or your parent who will look it over and declare it brilliant.

The major argument here is that the writers behind these models were nearly driven insane by their editor who kept sending back the draft, often with only miniscule steps forward toward the end product. Over ten days of constant back and forth, the following essay on Yeats' poem finally arrived at both clarity and power. So in the bleakest hours of a really wild night, hang in there: the essay can see the light of day.

Tia Ramos
New York University
November, 2015

The Resetting of the Cycle in "The Second Coming"

Yeats' poem, "The Second Coming," is hinged on the concept of "the gyre," a mathematical form of the movement of the "Spiritus Mundi," which literally translates to "world spirit," a spirit in which all people are connected through "the Great Memory" (Introduction to W.B. Yeats, *Norton Anthology*). This Spirit, seen in the "gyre," "cannot be fundamentally altered," and has the "inevitability of the tides" (Mann). According to Yeats, the gyre's spinning is just an "inevitable pattern," and at a certain argument in time and space, everything "falls apart" and the result is "mere anarchy"—the separation of the "falcon" and "the falconer." As this Spiritus Mundi falls apart and history spins out of control, the poem leads to an inevitable reset—some kind of rebirth.

It's funny that to get to this reset, you need chaos—you need everything to fall apart. The poem seems to say that there are two forces, forces in the human mind that have stopped working in conjunction with one another, what Carl Jung called the personal and then the collective unconscious—people themselves and History. The collective unconscious would act, then, as a personal link to larger forces outside of us that govern even our personal and individual beliefs. And as far as people go, the poem tells us who are the "best" and who are the "worst," and these two kinds of people are, perhaps, just part of our own minds—Jung's two forces. There is the part that we have to use to be in society ("the best," but who often "lack all conviction"), and there is the one that rebels but that is fully individual (ironically "the worst," as far as society is concerned). Perhaps Maud Gonne, the Irish revolutionary and Yeats' lover (the "worst" in society's eyes and the "best" in Yeats'), stands behind the ambivalence of the narrator, who can't seem to make up his mind, as it were, and thus "fall[s] apart."

We know from psychology that personal crisis—or falling apart—often leads to personal redemption. There is a reset at the bottom of our darkest times. We can snap out of it, but the poem starts to wonder what this snapping-out-of-it, this resetting, will look like. The poem finds a rough beast out there in the sands of our metaphoric deserts. It's a sphinx: the riddle-like thing that tormented Oedipus' Thebes that's also not too unlike the winged beasts of the four evangelists who foretell the end times—the Revelation in the *New Testament*. This time, a frightening yet somehow wise beast seems to be what we find in this instance of falling apart.

With such a creature, one wonders if this falling apart is going to be such a good thing. But regardless of whether it's a good thing or a bad thing, it's inevitable. This center "cannot hold"—it's collapsed and disintegrated. Just look at the recent Great War or the Russian Revolution to see a collapsed center. Those events were full of slogans that pushed only the historical self (the larger society) and just put the personal self (the individual) on the back shelf. Now, as the rough beast "slouches towards Bethlehem," "centuries" of violence and anarchy are simply repeating themselves. It's always been this same cycle, says the poem. This is just another resetting. But does it just keep going and going?

The poem says no. This cycle does, in fact, have an end. A judgment means that the gyre can no longer be allowed its repetition and "The Second Coming" is definitely not the same thing as, say, "The Thousandth Coming"—we only have two shots at this thing and this poem says we've blown the first. This is the Second Coming of Christ—judgment day. This insanity has come to an end. We humans never seemed to get it, and the poem says that our collective ego has caused this "revelation [that] is at hand." This struggle between the two kinds of people, the best and the worst, and the struggle between the two forces, the larger society and the individual, can no longer be sustained. This time, our self-created gyre will not reset.

Works Cited

Mann, Neil. "Geometry." *W.B. Yeats and "A Vision."*
http://www.yeatsvision.com/secondnotes.html. Web.

Yeats, W.B. "The Second Coming." *Norton Anthology of English Literature*. Eds. M. H. Abrams, et al. 6th ed. Vol. 2. New York: Norton, 1993. Print.

Bibliography

The following is a bare-bones list of books you'll want to own as you go forward in your writing practice. Of the hundreds of good writing manuals out there, these are some of the essentials.

Clements, Jessica, et al. *The Chicago Manual of Style, Sixteenth Edition.* Chicago: Univ. of Chicago Press, 2014.

Every professional editor has this reference book within arm's reach for every possible editing question. It's a must-own reference book for the pros. Writers of all levels will benefit from being able to look up the most minute detail.

Fowler, Ramsay, and Aaron, Jane, eds. *The Little, Brown Handbook, Fourteenth Edition.* New York: Longman, 2015.

The most easily navigable reference guide to grammar, mechanics, organization, and style in general. Applicable for secondary students all the way up to professional editors.

Goldberg, Natalie. *Writing Down the Bones: Freeing the Writer Within.* Boston: Shambhala Publications, 1986.

In chapters such as "Writing as a Practice, "Fighting Tofu," "Man Eats Car," and "The Power of Detail," Ms. Goldberg applies a Zen approach to the writing process with both humor and clarity.

Modern Language Association of America. *MLA Handbook, Eighth Edition.* New York: Modern Language Association Press, 2016.

The standard in research documentation. If you want to make sure you have the details right for your next academic research and publishing project, use this book.

Strunk, William, and White, E.B. *The Elements of Style*. New York: Macmillan, 1972.

The all-time classic. Your grandparents studied it, and so should you. Just a hundred pages long, this is the ultimate in concise handbooks on style. E.B. White wrote for The New Yorker for almost forty years, and most people agree that he created the magazine's unique and impeccable style. Look up and live by Rule #17: "Omit needless words."

Williams, David. *Sin Boldly: Dr. Dave's Guide to Writing the College Paper, 2nd Edition*. New York: Basic Books, 2004.

An excellent and funny guide to the standard-issue college paper. The concept here is about taking risks and not just following the pack. This is one of the few down-to-earth, tell-it-straight, how-to books on writing the engaging paper. Dr. Dave is in the trenches, teaching in a university writing program.

Made in the USA
Coppell, TX
01 May 2020

23562294R00089